101 Questions & Answers on
PRAYER

101 Questions & Answers on
PRAYER

Joseph T. Kelley

Paulist Press
New York/Mahwah, NJ

Cover design by Sharyn Banks
Book design by Lynn Else

Library of Congress Cataloging-in-Publication Data

Kelley, Joseph T., 1948–
    101 questions & answers on prayer / Joseph T. Kelley.
        p. cm.
    Includes bibliographical references and indexes.
    ISBN 978-0-8091-4561-4 (alk. paper)
    1. Prayer—Christianity—Miscellanea. 2. Prayer—Catholic Church—Miscellanea.
I. Title. II. Title: One hundred one questions and answers on prayer. III. Title: One hundred and one questions and answers on prayer.
    BV210.3.K46 2008
    248.3′2—dc22
                                                                    2008024485

Published by Paulist Press
997 Macarthur Boulevard
Mahwah, New Jersey 07430

www.paulistpress.com

Printed and bound in the
United States of America

Contents

PART FOUR: MEDITATION AND CONTEMPLATION

PART FIVE: PRAYER IN OTHER TRADITIONS

PART SIX: STRUGGLING TO PRAY

PART SEVEN: COMMITTING TO PRAYER

To Father Paul Keyes

Acknowledgments

Many friends and colleagues have helped, some unaware, in the writing of this little book by their encouragement, insights, corrections, and example. From Merrimack College I thank particularly Mark Allman, Kay and Gil DeBurro, Kevin Dwyer, OSA, Kathy Fitzpatrick, April Gagne, Rabbi Robert Goldstein, Helen Hanigan, Richard Hennessey, Victoria Izzo, Warren Kay, Barbara LaChance, Arthur Ledoux, Gary McCloskey, OSA, Georgianne Medor, Tim Montgomery, George Morgan, OSA, Porig O'Hare, Bridget Rawding, Steve Scherwatzky, and Jim Wenzel, OSA.

Many Augustinian brothers and sisters have nurtured my own prayer life over the years. I mention especially my early teachers Bob Andrews, OSA, Don Burt, OSA, and Joe Duffey, OSA; Brian Lowery, OSA, and Ian Wilson, OSA, in San Gimignano, Italy; and the contemplative nuns of the ancient Augustinian monastery at Lecceto near Siena.

My gratitude to my parents is deep and abiding; I hope that this book reflects in some measure the faith they shared and the prayers they taught. My wife Alina and children Kasia and Patryk also deserve immense thanks for their continuing love and support.

Dr. Christopher Bellitto of Paulist Press has been my editor for an accumulating number of years. His review and his vision continue to enrich my work. I am grateful for the grace of his intellectual and spiritual companionship.

Finally, I dedicate this book to Father Paul Keyes of St. Michael Parish in North Andover, Massachusetts. I am just one among the many for whom the deep faith, priestly ministry, and constant prayer of this loving Christian have made all the difference.

Joseph T. Kelley
August 28, 2007

Note on Scriptural Citations

Christian prayer is rooted in the Bible. Both the Old Testament (also called Hebrew Scriptures) and the New Testament inspire, enrich, and inform the theology and practice of Christian prayer. So the Bible is cited liberally throughout this text.

For those not familiar with how biblical citations are noted, the following may be helpful. When a particular passage from scripture is quoted or cited as relevant, the name of the biblical book is given, followed by the chapter, and then after a colon the verse or verses. Thus Exod 24:3 means the Book of Exodus, chapter 24, verse 3. Likewise, 2 Cor 2:3–10, 15 means the Second Letter to the Corinthians, chapter 2, verses 3 to 10 and also verse 15. A semicolon closes the chapter being cited and opens a new chapter. Thus Exod 19:18; 33:9 means the Book of Exodus, chapter 19, verse 18 and chapter 33, verse 9. I use the commonly accepted abbreviations for the names of biblical books.

The reader is encouraged to refer to the biblical passages cited for a deeper understanding of the origins of the scriptural and theological ideas presented here.

Introduction

Prayer is the raising of mind and heart to God or asking good things from God. This definition comes from the early centuries of the Christian church. Though simple and straightforward, behind this description of prayer lies a complex and profound experience. The purpose of this little book is to invite the reader, question by question, through the intricacies of praying toward deeper insight into the mysteries of prayer.

To survey the world of prayer, we will use several measures to guide our way and plot our progress. These include three common experiences that serve as analogies for interpreting the nature of prayer: conversation, presence, and memory. We will also discuss three vital faculties that we exercise while praying: feeling, intellect, and will. Finally, we will explore how prayer sanctifies or transforms three complementary human initiatives: giving and receiving, movement and stillness, interiority and ecstasy.

Three Analogies for Prayer: Conversation, Presence, and Memory

Three of our ordinary activities or everyday experiences provide analogies to help us understand the nature of prayer. These are conversation, presence, and memory. First of all, prayer can be thought of as conversation. In daily life we engage words to share with each other our ideas, feelings, and decisions. Through conversation acquaintances slowly become friends. In more significant exchanges we turn friends into confidants by revealing the deeper parts of ourselves. Conversation forms and fashions our relationships.

Prayer is conversation with God. It is an act of faith in the reality of a divine listener. Prayer is relating to God as one might to a friend or confidant. In prayer we use the vocabulary of everyday language to open up to God who, we believe, lovingly awaits our words. "From my mouth to God's ear," as the Yiddish proverb says. Whether we pray out loud with our mouths or express words silently in our mind and heart, prayer is trusting that God listens to what we have to say. Every prayer is a personal act of faith that furthers our relationship with God.

Prayer is presence. Often our relationships, especially the more mature ones, move beyond conversation. We can spend hours in silence enjoying the presence of a loved one. There is no need for talk. In analogous ways prayer can be simple, silent communion with God. We have no need to say anything, confident that God already knows what is in our heart and mind. At such times prayer is quiet dwelling in the presence of the Holy One.

Prayer is also memory. Every birthday celebration for a friend or family member, every card we send to commemorate a special date or event, each contact to let someone know we are thinking about him or her, all such efforts strengthen and deepen our relationships. It is essential that we build into our days and years many and varied ways of remembering those who mean so much to us. Memory is the essence of love.

Each time we pray, we exercise memory. We remember God. Just as we celebrate those whose lives are important to us in order that our relationships will deepen and grow, we also remember God so that our spiritual lives will intensify and expand.

Three Faculties Used in Praying: Feeling, Intellect, and Will

We will also refer to three essential human faculties or capacities that shape our praying: feeling, intellect, and will. Our definition of prayer includes raising one's heart to God. In prayer we can bring any and all of our feelings to God—love and hate, joy and sorrow, fear and anger, jealousy or envy, depression or boredom—anything that fills our heart. No feeling is unworthy of prayer nor of God who is the origin of our capacity to feel. Indeed, we are often drawn to prayer by and through our feelings.

Prayer also comprises intellect. Prayer is the lifting of the mind to God. In prayer we lay bare before God our thoughts, ideas, plans, deliberations, ruminations, dreams, and hopes. We reflect on the meaning of creation, of history, of current events, and of God's providence in the universe and in our lives. We mull things over in God's hearing, hoping that God's grace will clarify, deepen, and purify our thinking.

Sometimes we pray because a decision lies before us. We present our reflections and our feelings to God so that we may make the right choice. Thus prayer is often a request for wisdom. Like the psalmist, we ask God to "enlarge my understanding," "make me wiser," and "keep my steps steady" (Ps 119:32, 98, 133). Life's important decisions are frequently the occasions of grace that guide us back to prayer and nudge us once again toward God.

Prayer: The Sanctification of Human Initiative

The history of prayer is a history of human ingenuity. For millennia believers of all types have been sanctifying selected activities by drawing them into the orbit of prayer, making them "holy" or "set apart for God" in the process. We will emphasize three sets of such initiatives frequently associated with prayer: giving and receiving, movement and stillness, interiority and ecstasy.

Prayer provides the opportunity to give to God. Anyone or anything that we bring to prayer becomes a gift to God. When we remember a loved one as we pray, we present that person to God.

When we bring a worry, a request, a thought, or a hope to God, it becomes holy by being presented to the Holy One. Prayer transforms our words, our feelings, our decisions, and our requests into gifts that rise to God like the incense offered at the evening sacrifice in the Jerusalem Temple of old (Ps 141:2).

Just as prayer is giving to God, it is also receiving from God. Perhaps the most common prompt to prayer is a need, a request, a heartfelt call to God for help. We come to prayer with open, empty hands hoping that God will respond to us in our need and in our want. Prayer both prompts our initiative to give and purifies our readiness to receive.

Prayer inspires movement. Prayer, like love, moves beyond word and will to invade our body as well. The physical movements roused by prayer can be as simple as opening our hands in supplication, raising our arms in praise, bowing low in adoration, or kneeling in thanksgiving. Physical prayer can be complex as in the carefully practiced movements prescribed for *Salat,* the five daily prayers in Islam, or in the rituals of Catholic sacraments, or at the Seder meal of Passover.

Yet if prayer very often expresses itself in movement, it can sometimes mean stillness: "I have calmed and quieted my soul, like a weaned child with its mother; my soul is like the weaned child that is with me" (Ps 131:2). Prayerful stillness is an important dimension of religious traditions of the East. The various Hindu traditions of yoga, for example, provide sophisticated techniques for calming the devotee not only by slowing down the mind and heart, but also by reducing breathing and pulse rate. Prayer, then, sanctifies movement and stillness; it inspires dance and repose; it occasions motion and rest.

The final initiatives that will help us understand the nature of prayer are interiority and ecstasy. Prayer opens the door of our soul and gently pushes us within ourselves. It is an invitation to leave the world and its cares behind to enter into the presence of God within: "But whenever you pray, go into your room and shut the door and pray to your Father who is in secret; and your Father who sees in secret will reward you" (Matt 6:6).

Yet just as prayer can be a retreat into the soul, it can also be ecstasy, a going out of or beyond ourselves. We experience ecstasy in different ways in our lives. When we fall in love, we can completely lose our self in the reality of our beloved. Ecstasy is also a component of aesthetics. The beauty of a work of art or literature can transport us above and beyond ourselves by its power to inspire and elevate.

In prayer, ecstasy is a going beyond or outside of one's self and into the very mystery of God. All of the major religious traditions have orders, sects, or schools that foster this profound experience of abandoning the self and entering into the Spirit of God. We will consult them as guides in our exploration of prayer.

Grace

There is one final, essential idea that appears again and again throughout our study. It pervades all our analogies for prayer, infuses our vital faculties as we pray, and inspires the variety of our prayerful ingenuities. This is the doctrine of *grace*.

Prayer, in its deepest scriptural sense, is always a response to God. We speak to God because God first spoke to us in the Divine Word. We remember God because God never forgets us. We enter God's presence, because God was, is, and always will be present within and around us. God's endless initiatives of love toward us are called grace. All prayer is a response to grace, to God's infinite offers of love that surround and suffuse our being, that impregnate every moment of our time and invade every instant of our history.

This teaching of grace leads to the conviction that prayer is for everyone. God does not discriminate. God bestows infinite grace on all, and gives the gift of prayer equally to all. No matter what our religious standing or spiritual condition may be, we can still pray. Prayer is the prerogative of saint and sinner, of novice and veteran, of believer and agnostic, of child and elder, of the slow and the clever, of the healthy and the dying. Everyone can lift mind and heart to God or request good things of God. Even this book, with its 101 questions and answers, together with your queries and convictions about prayer are agents of God's grace, inviting us ever deeper into the mysterious encounter with the divine that we call prayer. So let's begin, in grace.

PART ONE
Prayer and Faith

1. What is prayer?

Research prayer and you will find a dizzying array of definitions and descriptions from all across the religious spectrum. We will use the classical definition of prayer that slowly emerged over the early centuries of Christian history: prayer is raising mind and heart to God or asking good things of God. Theologians like St. Augustine, St. Basil, St. John Damascene, and St. John Climacus all contributed to this understanding of prayer.[1]

This traditional Christian definition presents prayer as an active, hopeful, and flexible human endeavor. Prayer is active in that it is an act of the will, a choice. It is an intentional approach to God, a turning to or movement toward the Divine Being. As such, it is a fully human enterprise, available to anyone and everyone who chooses to open up mind and heart, intellect and feeling, thought and emotion to God. Prayer is a creative initiative, a courageous decision to greet the Infinite.

Our definition also implies that prayer is hopeful. Prayer acknowledges God as the origin of all good things who wants to give good things to all who ask (Matt 7:7–11). It recognizes our reliance upon a higher power who willingly receives our requests and who lovingly responds to them. In that sense prayer is not only hopeful, it is humble. It is an acknowledgment of our dependence upon God and an act of submission and surrender to a good and loving Creator.

Prayer in this approach is also flexible. It is not defined by or limited to specific, proscribed words or rituals. We can each lift our own mind and heart to God in our own way. These ways change and grow throughout the various stages of life. We all request different things of God as our circumstances change and our needs evolve over the course of a lifetime. This definition is also flexible in that it applies to the many and varied traditions of prayer across the world's religions throughout history. In an age when the members of different religions struggle to find commonalities amid their differences, this definition of prayer provides a helpful meeting point.

However, no matter how valuable a definition may be, we must actually practice prayer to grow in an understanding of this mystery. In many ways prayer is like a motor skill, such as riding a bike or playing a musical instrument. You can read about it, but you really don't know until you actually try it yourself.

2. Is prayer like talking to God?

Yes, we can understand prayer as conversation with God. However, it is important to note that God initiates the conversation. This may seem counterintuitive. Our experience in prayer is often that we do all the talking and wait for God to respond. Or that we have in fact not been doing much talking with God at all—perhaps for many years—and now have to find some way to begin an awkward conversation.

Yet most religions, especially Judaism and Christianity, understand prayer as a response to God's self-revealing love. We speak to God because God first spoke to Abraham (Gen 12; 15; 17), to Moses (Exod 3), to the prophets (Isa 6:6–13; Jer 1:4–13, Ezek 1:28—3:11), to Mary (Luke 1:26–56), and especially through Jesus, the Word of God (John 1:1, 14). Whenever, wherever, and however we enter the conversation, it is always in response to God who "first loved us" (1 John 4:19).

3. What can I talk to God about?

About anything. In prayer we can share our thoughts (even the less noble ones), our feelings (even the embarrassing ones), or our decisions (even our indecisiveness). Prayer is not a matter of presenting God with fine ideas, holy sentiments, and perfect manners. We can bring to God our "broken spirit" (Ps 51:17). God prefers "an open ear," attentive to the Divine Word more than any impressive sacrifice or costly offering (Ps 40:6–8). Prayer is less the etiquette of diplomatic conversation with royalty, and more a family exchange in which we are as honest as possible in speaking and as open as possible in listening.

Whatever we bring to God is blessed by our bringing it. Whatever we talk to God about becomes a kind of sacrifice that is transformed and made sacred by God's receiving it. We can bring anything to our conversations with God.

4. But if God is all knowing, what's the purpose of expressing my thoughts or feelings to a Divine Being who already knows them?

It's true that God already knows what is in our mind and heart: "O LORD, you have searched me and known me. You know when I sit down and when I rise up; you discern my thoughts from far away" (Ps 139:1–2). However, prayer is less for God and more for us.

Ordinary, everyday conversation with family or friends often helps us realize what we are thinking. The exactness of expression excavates what has been buried within us, hidden from our immediate awareness. Words shared with another help bring into sharper focus ideas or feelings or decisions that we first perceive only in faint outlines. How do I know what I think or what I feel until I hear what I say?

In the same way prayer as conversation with God helps us discover what may be difficult for us to understand or admit about ourselves: "You desire truth in the inward being; therefore teach me wisdom in my secret heart" (Ps 51:6). Our conversations with God help us find words that lead us to our inward being and to the truth of our secret heart. Through prayer God helps us listen to our own mind and heart so that we gradually grasp the deeper truths about ourselves that are revealed in and through our very praying.

5. Can I use my own words to pray?

Certainly. Religion is natural to human beings. St. Augustine reminds us at the beginning of his *Confessions* that we are created to be in relationship with God: "You have made us and drawn us to yourself, and our heart is unquiet until it rests in you."[2] So we can speak to God with the sentiments of our own hearts. We can approach the Holy One in the sanctuary of our own minds. We can use our own words to express our natural, heartfelt, inner desire to seek God.[3]

Yet most of us are first tutored in prayer by the religion in which we were nurtured and raised. Just as we learn the language, customs, and morals of our culture, most of us are also taught how to pray. We receive prayers to repeat and memorize. These prayers and rituals, which were learned from family and religious teachers, can support and develop our natural desire for God. They can guide, shape, and encourage our praying.[4]

However, we do not have to be limited to the formal prayers we learned as children. Just as studying poetry makes us better poets in our own right, learning the basic prayers of our faith prepares us to approach God through our own words. We can also mix the words and phrases of prayers that we have received from scripture and from our religious tradition with the thoughts and feelings that originate in our own mind and heart. Faith arises from both nurture and nature. So, too, our prayer emerges from the formulas we repeated in religious school, as well as from the words we collect for God out of our own ingenuity and inquiry.

6. Can I pray without any words at all?

Yes. As we have seen, the analogy of conversation can help us understand the nature of prayer. However, there are times when we stutter and stumble before God, when we hesitate and halt, unable to express ourselves. Our feelings may be so strong or so ambivalent that we have trouble putting them into words for God. For example, we can sometimes be enveloped by a happiness that surpasses verbal expression; words fail to capture our joy. By contrast, on occasion we may be so angry about something that all we can do is sputter. Sometimes sorrow or grief may get only as far as a wordless groan. Or anxiety over an important decision may have us

so confused that we can hardly articulate the options that are spin-
ning around in our brains. At such times our effort, even our frus-
tration, is itself prayer.

The psalmist reminds us that the efficacy of our prayer does
not depend on our ability to be eloquent. God already knows what
is in our heart: "Even before a word is on my tongue, O LORD, you
know it completely" (Ps 139:4). St. Paul also addresses this inabil-
ity to find the right words to express ourselves clearly to God:
"Likewise the Spirit helps us in our weakness; for we do not know
how to pray as we ought, but that very Spirit intercedes with sighs
too deep for words. And God, who searches the heart, knows what
is the mind of the Spirit" (Rom 8:26–27). Our ability to pray does
not depend on our capacity for eloquence. Even the most inartic-
ulate of prayers are precious to God.

Prayer can be wordless in another way, less conflicted than
just described. Sometimes we just want to spend time with God.
We may have nothing particular to say, but feel a desire to remember God's presence. The psalmist calls this desire simply wanting to
"behold the face of God" (Ps 42:2), or quietly to "ponder your
[God's] steadfast love" (Ps 48:9). This type of silent or quiet prayer
is called contemplation. We will discuss it further in question 61.

7. Do I need to pray every day?

If we think of prayer as a relationship, we can ask this question
in a different way: how often should I converse with God to deepen
our relationship? We know that good and regular communication
strengthens the important relationships in our lives. Marriage,
friendship, and family all require some kind of ongoing communication to continue growing and deepening. On the other hand,
failure to communicate weakens a relationship and can even doom
it to failure.

Our relationship with God also requires communication.
True, prayer is less for God's benefit and more for ours, as we discussed in question 4. God is not dependent on my self-revelation
in the same way as my spouse or friend. However, regular prayer

makes our relationship with God a real part of our lives. The prayerful expression of our mind and heart to God changes us, little by little, day by day. As we continually lift our thoughts and feelings to God, as we ask for good things from the loving Creator, the power of prayer transforms the way we think and feel and choose. We become more conscious of the abiding reality of God in our lives. Daily prayer reminds us of God's presence and work in our lives.

Prayer is also a counterweight to the many inner tendencies and outer distractions that pull us away from God, dull our awareness of the divine, and lull us into a self-centered life that takes little account of the Creator. The Book of Hebrews challenges us to "lay aside every weight and the sin that clings so closely," and to "run with perseverance the race that is set before us, looking to Jesus the pioneer and perfecter of our faith" (Heb 12:1–2). Prayer, like the training of an athlete, is necessary for an enduring, invigorating life of faith. Without prayer we can soon grow sluggish, slow, and discouraged. St. Ignatius of Loyola called his program of prayer *Spiritual Exercises*. This former soldier knew that progress in faith requires regular training, dedication, and practice.[5]

So should we pray every day? It depends on how real we choose to make our life of faith; how strong we want to grow in faith; how far we want to journey along the way with Jesus the pioneer; and how prepared we hope to be, with God's grace, for the difficulties and trials that await us along the way.

8. What if I forget to pray?

With all the pressures and responsibilities of life, it is easy to forget God. The Old Testament is filled with laments over Israel's forgetfulness: "But they soon forgot his works....They forgot God, their Savior, who had done great things in Egypt" (Ps 106:13, 21). In the same way we can very quickly forget God and live as if God did not matter. Without prayer, faith becomes an absentminded abstraction outside the sphere of daily life, having little influence on it.

However, if on any given day we forget to pray, or even if we go many weeks or months without praying, God will always call us back by the promptings of grace. As we emphasized in question 2, God initiates the conversation of prayer. Even when we might forget God for a while, God never forgets us (Isa 49:15; Matt 10:29–31; Luke 12:6–7).

9. How can I know God listens to me when I pray?

Every prayer is in itself an act of faith, a statement of confidence in God's readiness to listen and respond. Yet faith is not knowledge (1 Cor 13:12). Our prayer may sometimes be tentative, filled with hesitation or even skepticism. However, the fact that we even try to pray is itself a stirring of our belief, a willingness to give God the benefit of our doubt.

It is also helpful to remember that whenever we decide to pray, we step into an ancient march of faith. Our prayer enlists us into a long parade of believers that extends back through the ages. No act of prayer is its own origin. Every time we pray we remember. We recall God's love for the generations of those who have preceded us in faith—and doubt: "I remember the days of old, I think about all your deeds, I meditate on the works of your hands" (Ps 143:5). To pray to God in the present moment is to make an act of faith that the divine love is just as available here and now as it has always been, and always will be for God's people. Every time we pray we proclaim God's "steadfast love toward us," and declare that "the faithfulness of the Lord endures forever" (Ps 117:2).

10. But I have prayed for things in the past and did not get them. Why didn't God respond?

One way of understanding what seems to be a negative response from God is to distinguish between what we want and what we need. We often pray for things we want, but may not need. In fact, what we want may actually interfere with our receiving what we truly need. The Creator is attentive to our needs, even if we ourselves might remain unaware of them, and responds even if we ourselves fail to ask: "Therefore the LORD waits to be gracious to you; therefore he will rise up to show mercy to you" (Isa 30:18). It is not as if prayer initiates God's concern for us. Prayer rather prepares us to receive good things from God.

Every prayer of petition is an occasion to gain the wisdom to discern our true needs and to grow in prudence regarding our wants. Prayer is not a contract with God in which we specify what we want and stipulate how much we are willing to pray or pay in order to get it. Rather, prayer is a covenant to which God has called us and through which the Creator gives us all we need as creatures.[6] In prayer we put our needs and our wants before a loving God who always responds in ways that ultimately deepen that relationship. Prayer gradually tutors us in our needs and slowly stretches our imaginations to consider "what no eye has seen, nor ear heard, nor the human heart conceived, what God has prepared for those who love him" (1 Cor 2:9).

11. So is God really interested in what I have to say?

God is infinitely interested in what we say or what we can't yet bring ourselves to say. One of the most compelling images of God's almighty interest in us is found in the parable of the prodigal son (Luke 15:11–32). God is like the father in the parable who spends his days and nights watching for his renegade son, scanning the horizon for any sign of his return.

When the son finally appears in the distance, the father runs out to greet him as he approaches the homestead. He yearns to reveal to the wandering boy the great depth and breadth of his parental love. In preparing for his embarrassing return home, the prodigal son had practiced an initial conversation with his father, expressing his unworthiness and asking to be taken back as a hired hand. But, as Jesus tells the story, the son's rehearsed request is hardly out of his mouth when the joyful father, hugging and kissing his child, orders him immediately reinstated and commands a banquet be prepared in his honor. In this story Jesus gives us a glimpse of God's interest in us, in our prayer, and in our happiness.

12. This story of Jesus is very comforting. However, there are times when I feel more like the older son in the parable, overlooked by God despite my faithfulness. Why do I sometimes feel like God is ignoring me?

Prayer can sometimes be an experience of the absence of God. We may pour out our heart and soul to the Lord only to be met by empty silence. Our heartfelt desires or questions or petitions may rise up only to disappear into a cosmic black hole. God can seem remote, aloof, and disinterested. Even veteran churchgoers can sometimes feel adrift in their life of prayer, lost and fearful that their friendship with God has hit rocky, inhospitable shores.

This experience of God's absence is nothing new in the history of prayer. The psalmist cried: "Why are you so far from helping me, from the words of my groaning? O my God, I cry by day, but you do not answer; and by night, but find no rest" (Ps 22:1–2); "Why, O LORD, do you stand far off? Why do you hide yourself in times of trouble?" (Ps 10:1). In such times our prayer may feel like empty, wordless waiting. We become rather like the anxious father in Jesus' parable—bereft of the beloved, abandoned, and even rejected.

The demands of life often separate us from loved ones. Students get homesick when they first leave family and friends for a distant college or a first job. Parents suffer the empty nest syndrome. Lovers are separated by war. Friends grow apart because of physical or political or psychological distance. The circumstances of life are so contingent and variable, so fragile and unpredictable, that we can find ourselves suddenly isolated, remote, or exiled from persons and places that once filled us with joy.

The life of prayer is no different. There will be times when our feelings, our thoughts, our decisions, or simply the circumstances of our lives affect a sense of distance or separation from God. At such times faith instructs us that, however we might feel, God is still present, still close, still more intimate to us than we are to ourselves, as St. Augustine reminds us.[7] Our prayer then becomes an exercise in patience: "Wait for the LORD; be strong, and let your heart take courage; wait for the LORD!" (Ps 27:14). At such times hope assures us that even this experience of God's absence works for our good (Rom 8:28). Our waiting itself becomes an opportunity for grace that fashions our minds and informs our hearts in ways that we cannot fathom. At such times love promises that nothing, even a sustained experience of divine silence, can separate us from the love of God (Rom 8:39). If our intention is to pray, then even the felt absence of God is itself prayer.

13. Sometimes I pray when I have to make an important decision. Is that a good idea?

There are some commonsense guidelines to making good decisions: (1) Get all the information you can about your options. (2) Listen to your mind and heart. (3) Consider the impact of your decision on others and the common good. (4) Don't decide on something when you are either too depressed or, for that matter, too exhilarated. Prayer can help with the last three.

As we discussed in question 4, prayer can help us come to a better and deeper knowledge of ourselves, of what we truly think and really feel. Bringing our issues and decisions to God provides a unique opportunity to reflect on them as well as to ask God's guidance. Prayer also provides time to consider how our choices and decisions might help or hurt others. In prayer we move out of and beyond ourselves toward God. In the light of faith we gain wider perspectives and begin to see things from something other than our own viewpoint so our choices are likely to be more circumspect and encompassing.

Prayer also tutors us in patience regarding decisions. Sometimes when we integrate prayer into decision making, we begin to appreciate the importance of knowing the right time to make a choice. Deciding becomes discernment when prayer tempers it with waiting and wisdom. The psalmist often speaks of prayer as waiting for God and divine enlightenment: "Do not let those who wait for you be put to shame....Lead me in your truth, and teach me...for you I wait all day long....May integrity and uprightness preserve me, for I wait for you" (Ps 25:3, 5, 21). Prayer can greatly enrich, strengthen, and deepen our decisions by helping us to listen to ourselves, to take account of others, and to wait for the best time to decide and act.

14. Does prayer make you a better person?

To the extent that prayer helps us make better decisions we could say yes, it contributes to our being a better person. Over time the habit of frequent, even daily, prayer makes us generally more reflective and so more likely to reach timely choices that are consonant with our values and more constructive of the common good. That's certainly a better way of living.

Beyond ethics and moral choices, however, prayer also makes us more genuine. If prayer helps us to live out of the deeper parts of our self, then it grounds us in authentic living. Prayer is a constant invitation to face the truth about oneself before God. A life of prayer can slowly tutor its practitioners to become honest, humble persons who have a realistic measure of themselves, "who walk blamelessly, and do what is right, and speak the truth from their heart" (Ps 15:2).

15. So will prayer keep me from sinning?

Sin is turning away from God, forgetting or ignoring God to the extent that we live as if God did not exist: "Fools say in their hearts, 'There is no God.' They are corrupt, they commit abominable acts" (Ps 53:1).

By contrast, prayer is remembering God. It is a deliberate insertion of time and space for God into our lives. However, a quick look at our own lives, or at the lives of many religious people—leaders and common folk alike—shows right away that prayer in and of itself does not keep us from sinning. Even though we pray regularly and earnestly, weakness often overtakes us: "The spirit indeed is willing, but the flesh is weak" (Mark 14:38; see also Matt 26:41). In the last petition of the Lord's Prayer, "lead us not into temptation," Jesus acknowledges and reminds us of our need for constant vigilance over our own sinful tendencies and those of others.[8] Prayer does not exempt us from the lure of lust. It does not free us of the weight of gluttony, greed, or sloth. Nor does it make us immune from destructive rage, insidious jealousy, or arrogant pride. St. Teresa of Avila reminds us that temptations to such vices can even interrupt our conversation and communion with God and "make war on the soul in this state of prayer."[9]

Prayer, however, can help us gradually grow in virtue. When we put time aside to remember God and make space for divine grace in our lives, we change little by little. In prayer we encounter the truth about God and ourselves. Over time this encounter with truth tempers our conceit, assuages our envy, and calms our wrath. The joy of prayer alleviates our addictions and rejuvenates our diligence. The intimacy of prayer purifies our love.

Prayer is not magic. It is not a supernatural charm that protects us from the evil within ourselves, nor is it an amulet that wards off the danger that threatens us from without. Prayer is a choice to remember and return to God as often as we want or need. In prayer we intentionally enter into and receive the grace of God that is always there for us, helping us, as St. Paul advises, to be renewed in the spirit of our minds, and to clothe ourselves with the new self, created according to the likeness of God in true righteousness and holiness (see Eph 4:23–24).

16. I often think about God, but how do I know when I am really praying?

Well, even just thinking about God can be a prayer. When we think about a loved one, we are deepening our relationship with her or him. Remembering or thinking about God can do the same. We can, however, note three things that distinguish prayer.

The first is intention. Just the simple decision to pray, the intention to lift our mind and heart to God, is already the beginning of prayer itself. Busy parents often get interrupted by kids just when they try to grab a few minutes of quiet to pray. Or the phone rings right as we plan to snatch a moment for reflection. God knows and receives our intention as a loving sacrifice, even if unavoidable obstacles intrude and disrupt our prayer. In his still popular book, *An Introduction to a Devout Life*, St. Francis de Sales (1567–1622) advised the people of his day how to be attentive to and intentional about daily prayer amid a busy life. His insights and advice about the decision to pray continue to enrich the lives of many ordinary Christians.

Prayer is also distinguished by reflection. Though distractions are inevitable, prayer requires some element of reflection. Just as careful attention to the other person makes for good conversation, prayer involves turning our minds and hearts away from other things to God. Prayer entails constructing a way to focus on God. That focus may be burning white hot to the exclusion of all distractions, as in deep meditation or contemplation (see questions 52–62). Or we may drift in and out of attention to God on many different levels. One way or another, prayer requires reflection.

The third dimension of prayer is interiority. Prayer is turning to God. This usually involves turning within. St. Augustine emphasized interiority as the essence of prayer: "O God, you are the light of my heart, bread for the inward mouth of my soul, the virtue wedded to my mind and the innermost recesses of my thought."[10] In many ways our prayer is a response to God dwelling within us, calling to us from within ourselves. Divine inwardness appears in many religious traditions. The Hindu scriptures describe God as the "Infinite Self within the lotus of the heart."[11] The Book of Deuteronomy proclaims that God's Word is "very near to you; it is in your mouth and in your heart" (Deut 30:14). In Islam one of the ninety-nine names of God is "The Inward" *(al-Batin)*. God dwells within us because God is within all things and has full knowledge of them (Qur'an LVII, 3).

How do you know when you are praying? When you intend to pray, reflect on God's presence and go within your own soul, then you have entered the mystery of prayer, whether it be for a brief, distracted moment, or for deep, extended contemplation.

PART TWO

Prayer and Religion

17. Are the official rituals and ceremonies of religion considered prayer?

Yes. Like private prayer, they are also occasions to lift mind and heart to God and to ask good things of God. At their best, the ceremonies and sacraments of a religious tradition are invitations to prayer. Most religious rituals begin with a call to prayer of some kind. Jewish prayer always begins with a blessing that reminds gathered worshippers to honor God as the source of every good thing: "*Baruch Atah Adonai*—Blessed are you, O God." Christian worship begins by inviting the assembly to enter God's presence through Christ and the Holy Spirit to pray: "In the name of the Father, and of the Son, and of the Holy Spirit." In Islam the call to "Come to Prayer" or *adhan* rings out five times each day proclaiming "*Allahu Akbar*—God is Great and is worthy of worship."

Ritual forms of public prayer, developed over centuries of practice and tradition, call members of the community together to share their faith and to support each other in giving praise and thanks to God.

18. Are the official prayers of a religion better or more powerful than private prayers?

No one can measure the relative value or power of any prayer, public or private. Prayers are received by the Holy One whose infinity renders all human measurement or comparison irrelevant. God's thoughts about prayer are not ours; God's ways of evaluating prayer are not ours (Isa 55:8–9). Jesus hints at the divine perspective when he comments on the greater value of the widow's small offering in the temple (Luke 21:1–4). So it's not a matter of official religious prayer or ritual being better than private prayer, just different.

19. What's the main difference between public prayer and private prayer?

The difference, of course, is that in public prayer we are pray-ing with others rather than alone. We can make a further distinc-tion: the difference between the official rituals of an established religious tradition, and the more informal, unofficial gatherings of believers who simply want to pray together.

These latter informal prayer groups involve members of the same faith, or even of different faiths, who gather informally to lift mind and heart to God, or to ask good things of God. Examples of such occasions include prayer breakfasts, ecumenical or interfaith prayers for peace, or memorial services for the deceased. Through shared words, silent meditation, or certain gestures, members of such prayer groups honor each other's faith and support each other's relationship with God. Such gatherings can be of great value for the participants and for their life of prayer.

These informal occasions for prayer are different from a reli-gion's official or liturgical forms of worship. The weekly celebra-tion of Sabbath and the annual observances of Yom Kippur, Rosh Hashanah, and Passover reflect millennia of tradition and express the deeply held beliefs and long-shared values of Judaism. The Catholic Mass or Christian worship and sacraments embody the ancient faith of the Church in Jesus as Lord and Savior and the gift of the Holy Spirit. The five daily prayers of Islam and the rigors of the month of Ramadan reveal Muslim submission to God and dedication to universal brotherhood and sisterhood. The great vari-ety of belief, devotion, and divinity in Hinduism is expressed in the diversity of its many ritual practices.

When we enter into the official rituals of a religion, the lan-guage, symbols, movements, music, dress, scents, and gestures cel-ebrated in that tradition all work together to form and shape the character of the common prayer. The result of an effective ritual is that participants lift their minds and hearts to God in union with each other. Their prayer together reflects the ways that their particular religious tradition conceives of God, relates to God, and approaches God.

20. So can public prayer with others help me in my private prayer?

Yes. Both the official religious rituals of our faith tradition as well as the more informal occasions of shared prayer can provide powerful faith experiences that enrich our personal prayer. Conversely, the time we spend in personal, private prayer can prepare us to enter into the public prayer more fully. The prayers we say in the privacy of our homes or the secrecy of our hearts and the shared prayers we join complement each other.

21. Is it wrong to get bored with or distracted during official ritual prayers?

No, it's not wrong. There could be many valid reasons why formal religious worship turns a person off. Sometimes we are painfully aware of hypocrisy in formal religion. Jesus comments on this: "And whenever you pray, do not be like the hypocrites; for they love to stand and pray in the synagogues and at the street corners, so that they may be seen by others" (Matt 6:5). In the same passage he reminds us that formal worship can become repetitive, wordy, and meaningless: "When you are praying, do not heap up empty phrases as the Gentiles do; for they think that they will be heard because of their many words" (Matt 6:7). Unfortunately the official prayers of any religion can become empty gestures, meaningless symbols, and self-serving sounds.

Also, our life of personal prayer is not static. It is more like a journey that passes through many different terrains, both low valleys and high mountains. We can spend time in dry, desert periods or plod dutifully across wide open and seemingly endless plains. Sometimes public, liturgical worship is a vibrant, welcome support to our own personal prayer life, building us up when we feel weak or vacillating. At other times formal religious services can become difficult to attend and even distracting to our faith. It is often hard to discern how our personal and public prayer lives should be integrated. However, to abandon altogether the common worship of one's religious tradition is a serious decision not to be taken lightly. At the very least such a decision deprives the community of the prayerful insight and faith witness of the one who has left.

22. Why are some religious services more attractive or inspiring than others?

Some communities put much thought, care, and resources into their worship services. Other communities do not. One can usually tell very quickly how much a priority common worship is to a congregation by attending its services. Ritual involves language, symbol, and movement. As such, aesthetics are important for good ritual. Beautiful language and music, cherished symbols, careful movement, and gracious gesture can all combine to help lift mind and heart to God. Careless, sloppy, unsightly, and discordant ritual is more likely to produce a prayerful request to God that the whole thing ends—soon.

Effective rituals do not have to be expensive or elaborate. Beauty, simplicity, and honesty can all come together in powerful common prayer. Good rituals, beautifully celebrated, communicate the beliefs and values of the faith they celebrate. Rituals have often been the occasion of conversion for people who experience divine grace through the shared worship of believers.

23. As a child I learned and memorized certain prayers from my religion. Can I use them now as an adult?

Most of us learned the basic prayers of our faith as children. Some of them were prayers specifically for childhood: "Now I lay me down to sleep…." Others were the formal prayers or blessings of our faith tradition learned from church ceremonies, religious teachers, or our family.

As we move along the journey of faith, we learn other prayers, perhaps more elaborate and eloquent. We may also use prayers from other religious traditions that help us express what we are experiencing deep within our life of faith. However, the prayers we learned in our earliest years are often the ones to which we return in difficult circumstances. Like our regional accent and family traits, these prayers emerge from the deepest layers of neural activity.

There are times when we find those simple, yet profound prayers we learned as youngsters very comforting. Under conditions of extreme stress, we all tend to revert to ways of relating and coping that characterized our childhood. Combat scenes from war films often portray soldiers who are under fire on the battlefield reverting to childhood prayers like the Hail Mary or Psalm 23, "The Lord is my shepherd...." These are dramatic examples of the psychological power of the prayers we learned in childhood.

As we age we also can grow to appreciate the wisdom and depth of these simple formulas that were the first to help us lift our mind and heart to and ask good things of God.

24. Is it better to kneel when praying?

In one sense it doesn't make any difference at all what posture we assume to pray. God hears us however we raise mind and heart in prayer. On the other hand, prayer involves the total person, body and soul, so posture, gesture, movement, and the engagement of our senses can help us enter prayer and sustain us in prayer.

The official rituals of religion teach us different ways of engaging the body in prayer. The Catholic Mass, for example, uses many postures, gestures, and sensual experiences: walking together in procession, standing together with open hands in common prayer, sitting while listening to scripture, standing to honor the words of the Gospel, kneeling in adoration and thanksgiving, shaking hands or embracing others in peace, signing oneself with the cross, smelling incense, and enjoying liturgical colors. African Catholics also make extensive use of ethnic or tribal dance in the liturgy.

Jewish ceremony also involves the body and its senses. Every Friday evening the Sabbath begins as the family table is set with wine and bread. The woman of the house then lights the two Sabbath candles, welcomes the Sabbath by waving her hands over the candles with eyes closed, and invokes God's blessing on the flame.

The five daily prayers of Islam require an elaborate, beautiful, and ascetic ritual of repeated kneeling, bowing, and prostration that envelops the worshipper in the act of prayer. The whirling dervishes of the Sufi tradition in Islam show how circling and twirling can bring the dancer to ecstatic union with God.

Such official rituals provide a rich source of examples or best practices that we can each work into our private prayer to help us grow in our life of prayer. We can take the practices of our own tradition or enrich them with gesture and movement from other traditions to develop our own style and manner of praying.

25. Is God more likely to hear my prayers when I pray in a sacred place like a church?

No. God is everywhere, dwelling even in the depths of our souls. The question is more about how space and place might help us recollect ourselves and enter prayer more fully. Sometimes we feel drawn to a sacred place like a church or shrine or temple to pray. Or maybe we feel closer to God in a place of natural beauty, such as walking deep in a forest or sitting on rocks above the ocean. Such spatial promptings to prayer are important to follow.

It is also helpful to designate a place in our homes that we regularly use for daily prayer. We can enhance that place with the Bible or a symbol or sacred object that can help invite and draw us into prayer.

26. What's the purpose of holy objects like rosary beads?

The Catholic Rosary developed in the Middle Ages as a prayer for the common folk in place of the Liturgy of the Hours or Divine Office, which by then had grown into an elaborate and complicated monastic ritual. The Rosary combines an Our Father and ten Hail Marys for each of fifteen decades. Each decade invites the one praying to move from bead to bead, repeat the associated prayer, and meditate on an event from the life of Jesus or Mary.

Prayer beads of many types are also found in other world religions. Hindus and Buddhists use them to repeat mantras and prayers. Muslims use them to count the ninety-nine names of God or to repeat the prayer Glory to God thirty-three times. In every tradition prayer beads or rosary beads are another way of engaging the body, calming the mind, and lifting the heart to God in meditation and prayer. They show how human ingenuity in many cultures engaged the body in prayer with the aid of a simple hand-held string of beads.

27. Do prayers "count" when we say them without thinking about them, for example, when we constantly repeat the Hail Mary while saying a Rosary?

In question 16 we talked about three things that make prayer what it is: intention, reflection, and interiority. Perhaps the most important of these is intention. We often get distracted in prayer, either by what's going on around us or by our own thoughts and feelings that pester us from within. When we catch ourselves daydreaming, worrying, solving problems, nodding off, or telling someone off, we need only gently renew our intention to lift mind and heart once again to God. The intervening moments are not dismissed or discounted by God who knows that "the spirit indeed is willing, but the flesh is weak" (Matt 26:41).

28. What about the practice of "offering up" an everyday chore or task to God; is that prayer?

Yes and no. Yes, in that we can offer our daily work or chores to God by simply making the intention to do so. They become a sacrifice to God because we intentionally set them aside for God. This devotion has been expressed in the Catholic prayer often referred to as one's Morning Offering.

But if we keep to our definition of prayer as lifting mind and heart to God or asking good things of God, then no. Prayer and work are different. In his famous monastic rule St. Benedict emphasizes a healthy daily balance of prayer *(orare)* and work *(laborare),* but he never identifies the two as the same. In fact he differentiates them clearly in the monastic schedule. In our contemporary workaholic society, we have to be careful about "baptizing" work and calling it prayer. Such an approach can be an excuse to avoid prayer. With the pressure of making money or advancing our careers, we can easily ignore the discipline of stopping work and putting our responsibilities and duties aside so that we might intentionally remember, praise, and thank our Creator.

Various religious practices help us keep this balance. Orthodox and Conservative Jews observe the Sabbath as sacred time during which work is prohibited. Muslims interrupt their work with the five daily prayers or *Salat.* In the West, however, the "Protestant work ethic" has tended to erode the sacredness of Sunday, leaving Christians of all denominations somewhat adrift in their efforts to sanctify certain times for prayer.

29. Is sacrifice prayer?

Yes, sacrifice can be a kind of prayer. Literally the word *sacrifice* means to "make holy." We sacrifice something when we set it aside for God, or dedicate it to God, thereby making it holy.

The history of religion is filled with endless examples of sacrifice—some inspiring, some horrifying. The first crops harvested from the fields, the best and unblemished animals from the flock, precious stones or artifacts, even first-born children have all been "set aside for God," sometimes by sacrificial death. The essence of sacrifice, however, is not destruction or death. It is rather the act and intention of setting aside something of value and designating it for God.

Thus each morning we can offer up or dedicate our whole day and all its toil to God. Our time and energy are things of value that we can sacrifice to God simply by making the intention to do so. Or we can take the fruits of our labor and set them aside for God by dedicating them in ways that benefit others, especially those who may need such benefit. We can give up certain food and drink for a period of time as Christians might in Lent, as Muslims do during Ramadan, and as Jews do for Yom Kippur. These are all examples of sacrifice, of setting things aside in different ways to remember, honor, petition, thank, and praise God.

Sacrifice then is prayerful when the sacrificial action involves raising mind and heart to God or asking something good of God. Sacrifice is a form of embodied prayer. One's prayerful intention extends out into the fields of labor and across the customs of culture in ways designed to remind us of God while we work, while we take refreshment, or as we relate to others. Sacrifice is a very simple, and at the same time, a very sophisticated kind of prayer. Whether it be something like the "widow's mite"—a secret and solitary offering of money made to benefit others—or whether it be the grand, worldwide observance of the sunrise to sunset fast during the month of Ramadan, sacrifice is a powerful example of prayerful faith. The essential feature of sacrifice that makes it prayer is the inner intention and direction of mind and heart to God that gets expressed and symbolized in the outward action.

30. Can activities like art or music or craft be considered prayer, even if God is not the obvious focus?

Many human activities can be occasions of grace that turn us toward God. Enjoying a piece of music, entering into a work of art, or exercising one's own God-given talent, skill, or craft can move our minds or raise our hearts to God. Prayer arises out of such activities when they open a conversation with God, or make us aware of the Divine Presence, or remind us of the divine love that is our origin and destiny.

The craft of the artist is especially inclined to prayer in that art is the quintessentially creative act. In a sense every work of art—every creative, artistic human endeavor: music, painting, sculpture, architecture, woodworking, writing, or illustrating—is by its nature akin to the divine dynamic of bringing a new form to reality and a new reality to form. When the artist becomes conscious of this spiritual dimension of art, and enters or embraces it, then prayerfulness imbues the artistic exercise of mind and heart.

The holy icons of Orthodox Christianity uniquely express and embody this intersection of art and prayer. To create these two-dimensional depictions of Christ, Mary, and the various saints and angels, the artist must take the time to prepare by prayer and fasting. The very execution of the work itself is considered an extended devotional act of prayer. The sole purpose of the finished work is to raise the minds and hearts of those who encounter it to God.

31. Do people pray to icons or religious images?

Remember that our definition of prayer is raising mind and heart to God or asking good things of God. An icon, image, statue, or any other kind of religious symbol is not itself the object of prayer. It is an aid to prayer. Such symbols invite worshippers into relationship with God by helping them lift mind and heart to the Holy One.

Hollywood portrayals of primitive religious rituals often leave the impression that tribal peoples actually worship some religious artifact, mountain, or animal. However, careful anthropological studies have often shown ancient and indigenous peoples to be much more sophisticated about approaching the divine through their symbols.

It's true that idolatry—mistaking the religious symbol for the divine itself—has corrupted religious practice at times in almost every tradition. Judaism and Islam have been especially cautious about the human tendency to short circuit worship by fixating on the religious symbol, exaggerating its importance, and mistaking its role. So these religions are much more restrictive in allowing or tolerating icons or images. On the other hand, Christianity and Hinduism celebrate the divine presence in creation through many and various symbols and abound with religious representations. The proper role of religious images, pictures, statues, and icons is to help raise our minds and hearts to God and to invite us to ask good things of the one and only God.

32. Can writing or journaling be considered prayer?

Yes. We can use writing or journaling as a way to express our thoughts and feelings to God. If we punctuate our writing with pauses for reflection and meditation, this can be a very prayerful practice.

If we allow ourselves to imagine how the various authors of the sacred scriptures did their writing, we can understand their efforts as inspired and prayerful. Their writing was a lifting of mind and heart to God. Likewise, our reading of their work inspires us to approach the Holy One.

33. Can reading a nonreligious text or listening to secular music be a form of prayer?

Yes. Again to the extent that a book or article or piece of music opens our mind and heart to God or moves us to ask God for help, it becomes an occasion of grace and an opportunity for prayer.

In Catholic theology this tendency to see God's loving grace as operative in and through all creation is called the *sacramental principle*. Because all of creation is God's work, it carries the divine reflection. Just as any work of art reflects the style and the passion of the artist, in an analogous way creation reveals the imprint of the Creator. So any part of creation can effectively call us into communion with the Source of all that is. One might even argue that the more artistically sophisticated a person becomes, the more aware of the dynamics of beauty and the principles of aesthetics, the more sensitive that person is to the divine power that sustains the structure and strength of art.

34. Can the study of science be an occasion of prayer?

Certainly. Just as the aesthetics of art can inspire our minds and hearts, so too can the beauty and balance and mystery of the laws of the universe become prompts to prayer, especially to adoration and thanksgiving. There are many eminent scientists who write about how physics leads to metaphysics; about how the intricacies of living organisms open up questions concerning the mystery of life; about how the immense complexity and interdependence of the chemical properties of the universe invite reflection on the meaning of existence itself. For many religious persons, the study of science often lifts mind and heart to God. Whereas the methods of science involve empirical observation, controlled experimentation, and careful prediction, the questions it considers often lead to the broader vistas of faith and prayer.

The contemporary British physicist-priest John Polkinghorne thinks that science challenges believers to situate their faith and prayer in the context of the universe itself. He reminds us that the world's religions have arisen during the last few thousand years or so, while the universe itself is fifteen billion years old. The questions and theories of science can stretch the breadth of our faith and deepen the profundity of our prayer.

PART THREE
Christian Prayer

35. Do Christians pray to Jesus or to God?

Both. Christians believe that in Jesus of Nazareth, God became human and shared fully in human history and destiny. This basic and fundamental Christian conviction that Jesus is the Son of God has profound implications for the nature of their prayer. In fact, Christian faith impacts the very dynamic of prayer as we have defined it.

When Christians lift mind and heart to God, their act of faith always and immediately encounters the mind and heart of God revealed in Jesus. When Christians ask good things of God, they do so knowing that any possible request has been anticipated by God, who has already given the ultimate good: the fullness of divine love revealed in Jesus. For Christians all their praying is in one way or another shaped and fashioned by their belief in Jesus as the Word of God, the Son of God. All Christian prayer is in some way a response to the love of God revealed in Christ.

36. So if prayer is conversation with God, do Christians talk only to Jesus?

Christians believe in the Trinity. God is One and only One. Yet within this unity there is a dynamic trinity of persons. Jesus reveals the Father's love to us (John 14:8–14), and pours into our minds and hearts the Holy Spirit (John 14:16, 17, 26). That divine Spirit unites us with Jesus, and through Jesus with the Father. Through our faith in Jesus we share in the dynamic, infinite life of a triune God. So Christians pray to God the Father through Jesus by the power of the Holy Spirit.

In practice Christians find themselves praying at times directly to God the Creator, the Father/Mother of all. They know in faith that such prayer is infinitely efficacious because when they address the Father, they pray in union with the Son: "Very truly, I tell you, if you ask anything of the Father in my name, he will give it to you" (John 16:23).

At other times Christians pray directly to Jesus, as the first martyr Stephen did at his death: "Lord Jesus, receive my spirit" (Acts 7:59); and as Paul did at his conversion: "Who are you, Lord?" (Acts 9:5). Christians pray to Jesus because they believe "He is the reflection of God's glory and the exact imprint of God's very being, and he sustains all things by his powerful word" (Heb 1:3).

From the earliest centuries of the Church, Christians have also prayed to the Holy Spirit, the indwelling of God and the source of their prayer. Liturgical prayers to the Holy Spirit are found in both the Roman and Byzantine liturgies for the feast of Pentecost.

37. So to whom do Christians pray in the official, liturgical prayers of the Church?

The official, ritual prayers of Christians generally follow the pattern that is summarized at the end of the eucharistic prayer of the Catholic Mass: "Through Christ, with Christ, and in Christ, in the unity of the Holy Spirit, all glory and honor is yours, almighty Father, for ever and ever." Almost always the formal prayers of the Mass, such as the opening prayer, the prayer over the gifts, and the prayer after communion are also addressed to the Father, "through Jesus Christ your Son, the unity of the Holy Spirit." The liturgical prayers of most other Christian communions and denominations follow this same basic pattern of Christian prayer.

38. Do Catholics pray to the Virgin Mary?

The best way to understand Catholic devotion to Mary is to recognize that for Catholic, Orthodox, and many other Christians she is the perfect example of prayer. As we discussed, Christians pray to God through, with, and in Jesus, to whom they are united by the Holy Spirit. In Catholic teaching Mary, as Jesus' mother, was united more closely with Jesus than any other person. She conceived him by the power of the Holy Spirit (Luke 1:35). The same Spirit is the origin of the faith and holiness that make her the model Christian, totally dedicated to the will of the Father (Luke 1:38, 46–49).

So Catholics do not worship Mary or give her the praise that is due God alone. They revere, honor, and love her for who she is: the Mother of God who is the perfect example of Christian life and faith.[12] Catholics and other Christians pray in union with Mary, who in her own person represents the ideal of Christian prayer to God through Jesus by the power of the Holy Spirit. Many artistic and liturgical representations of Mary portray her in a posture of prayer or *orans*—with hands outstretched and open. Such Marian iconography is an invitation to join her in lifting our mind and heart and body and soul to God.

39. So I take it that Catholics don't pray to the saints?

No, they do not pray to the saints. Let's reflect for a moment on who or what a saint is. In the early centuries of Christianity, some people became well known for their holiness, especially those who suffered death rather than betray their faith in Christ. Thus many of the early martyrs were presumed by the faithful and often declared by church leaders to have entered full and eternal union with God. Gradually other people whose lives were examples of faith and holiness were also acclaimed as model Christians whom God surely received into heavenly glory upon their deaths. By the twelfth century the Catholic Church in Rome had developed an official process for declaring or canonizing such persons as saints.

So saints are Christian heroes. Their lives are held up as models for inspiration and imitation by other Christians. Many countries or ethnic groups or Christian movements have saints with whom people can identify and from whom they draw inspiration and encouragement. In a desire to raise up such heroes, Pope John Paul II canonized hundreds of local saints in many countries during the twenty-six-and-a-half years of his pontificate. Over the centuries some saints like Francis of Assisi from Italy, Thérèse of

Lisieux (the "Little Flower") from France, Martin of Porres from Peru, Elizabeth Seton from the United States, or in our own day Blessed Mother Teresa of Calcutta have become universally venerated by Catholics and Christians around the world.

All Christians—living and deceased—are united by their common gift of the Holy Spirit. So devotion to the saints is a way of exercising our communion with them, as well as of honoring their faith and striving to imitate it.[13] We do not pray to the saints. We pray in communion with them to God through Jesus. We can also ask them to pray or intercede for us to God.

40. Can you say more about this idea of interceding and its relationship with prayer?

Traditional Christian teaching about prayer recognizes five basic forms of prayer: blessing, petition, intercession, thanksgiving, and praise.[14] *Blessing*—also called *adoration*—is the basic movement of Christian prayer (and, for that matter, of Jewish and Islamic prayer). It is the simple recognition that God is God, the Source of all reality, and that we are God's creatures who are united with the Holy One by lifting our minds and hearts in prayer.

Petition grows out of blessing when we ask God for what we need, knowing that we depend upon God for our very existence. A very common prayer of petition is asking forgiveness of God for our sins—often called the prayer of contrition. *Intercession* is praying to God on behalf of another person or a group of people, as Jesus did and does for us (John 17). *Thanksgiving* is not only prayer we make in gratitude for petitions or intercessions granted, but also is the characteristic of Christian prayer in response to the outpouring of divine love in Jesus and the Holy Spirit. Thanksgiving or Eucharist (from the Greek word for thanksgiving) is the heart of Christian worship. Finally, completing the circle of prayer, *praise* is lifting our mind and heart to God not so much in petition or intercession or even because of a particular blessing, but simply because God is God and deserving of our constant joyful recognition.

Christians, then, ask the Virgin Mary and the saints to intercede for them with God, just as we can intercede for each other
with God. Catholic and Orthodox Christians believe that during
the Liturgy of the Eucharist all Christians—both living and
deceased—are united with Mary, the saints, and the angels in common thanksgiving and praise to God for the greatest gift of all:
divine love revealed in Jesus.

41. Hold on, what's that about angels?

Angels have been part of ancient Persian, Jewish, Christian,
and Islamic traditions for centuries. They are understood to be
incorporeal beings, created as we are for relationship with God. In
the Old Testament the prophet Isaiah sees angels during worship in
the Temple of Jerusalem (Isa 6:1–7). In the New Testament Book
of Revelation they worship in the new, heavenly Jerusalem (Rev 4;
8:3–5). The early Christians believed that angels worshipped with
them during the celebration of the Eucharist (1 Cor 11:10).[15] That
is why in Christian art angels are depicted in mosaics, frescoes, and
paintings as worshipping alongside members of the Christian community during the sacred liturgy.

In Christian theology angels are understood to live in perpet-
ual adoration of God and to give God unceasing praise (Luke
2:13–14; Heb 1:6). They also protect us on this Earth (Job
33:23–24; Ps 91:11–12; Matt 18:10; Heb 1:14) and intercede on
our behalf before God in heaven (Tob 12:12).

42. Catholics and others often speak of devotions of different types, such as to the "Sacred Heart of Jesus," or to Mary's "Miraculous Medal," or to "St. Jude." What kind of prayers are these?

Symbols such as the Sacred Heart of Jesus, or a particular
medal celebrating the Virgin Mary, or a special devotion to St. Jude,
who traditionally intercedes on behalf of those who have begun to
lose hope, are aids to prayer. In prayer we lift our mind and heart

to God. But we pray also with and through our bodies. Religious symbols that capture and express our longings for God can help us focus our minds on God and turn our hearts toward heaven. Catholicism is rich with colorful varieties of symbols and customs that over the centuries have arisen out of the various cultures of its many peoples across the globe. Prayer needs embodied signs and aids that enrich the life of faith. The many statues, paintings, and other representations of the saints in Catholicism are reminders that our prayer life is shared with a great variety of other believers throughout history.

43. What is a novena?

Novena comes from the Latin word for nine. To make a novena is to dedicate oneself to the daily repetition of a prayer or set of prayers for nine consecutive days. Usually this is for a particular petition or intercession. There are many traditional novenas that have developed in Catholicism, such as to the Holy Spirit, the Virgin Mary, St. Joseph, and many other saints. The tradition of the novena may have originated from the nine days the disciples spent in prayerful expectation between Jesus' ascension into heaven (the Feast of Ascension Thursday) and the descent of the Holy Spirit upon the disciples at Pentecost (Acts 1:6—2:4).

44. What are the indulgences associated with some Catholic prayers?

Indulgences emerged from the Church's belief that prayer is effective in purging the soul of sin and its effects. Whether we pray for the remission of our own sins or intercede on behalf of another, especially the deceased, such prayers of petition do win God's forgiveness and indulgence.

In official prayer books of the Catholic Church you may find at the end of a prayer a phrase or designation such as "Forty-Days Indulgence." This simply means that this particular prayer, fervently prayed, has been declared by the Church to be the equivalent of the effects of sincere prayer over the longer period of time. It is the Church's way to encourage the faithful to pray often, and to remind us that even a brief effort on our part, inspired by grace, stirs infinite effects in the depths of divine love.

A prayer noted to win "Plenary Indulgence" is believed to remove all the effects of sin that may await us after death in purgatory. Again, it is a pastoral affirmation of the power of prayer and the fullness of God's love revealed in Christ. Over the centuries the effects of sin corrupted even this pastoral practice of indulgences. The recitation of a certain prayer and the monetary gift of a specified amount to the Church were thought to guarantee a soul in purgatory entrance into heaven. The abuse of selling indulgences helped to precipitate the Protestant Reformation.

The Catholic Church teaches that indulgences associated with certain prayers and the effects of our intercessory prayers for the dead depend entirely on God's mercy revealed in Christ and cherished by the Church, not on any human effort or exercise.[16] Ultimately we cannot reduce the mystery of prayer to any quantitative value. In its own way the pastoral practice of granting indulgences celebrates this truth by reminding us that our measures of time and effort are infinitely relative to God.

45. Do Catholics use the Bible to pray?

Yes. Ever since the Protestant Reformation in the sixteenth century, the Bible has been an important part of prayer and devotion in Protestant tradition. The Second Vatican Council (1962–65) encouraged Catholics as well to discover the great treasury of prayers in the Bible.

Prominent among all the prayers in the Old Testament are the 150 psalms. They are used throughout the liturgy as the texts for processional and recessional hymns, as congregational responses to readings from scripture, and as communion songs. Catholics are also encouraged, like their Protestant sisters and brothers, to use the psalms in their daily prayers and devotions. The psalms are also the foundation for the Liturgy of the Hours.

46. What is the Liturgy of the Hours?

The Liturgy of the Hours, also called the Prayer of Christians or the Divine Office, is the cycle of five daily prayers in Catholic liturgy: morning prayer, daytime prayer, evening prayer, night prayer, and the prayer of readings that can be done at any time of day or night. Each of these five hours of prayer contains two or three psalms and a canticle (song) from the Hebrew or Christian scriptures, along with readings from scripture and prayers of petition and intercession. The Song of Zechariah (Luke 1:68–79) at morning prayer, the Song of Mary (Luke 1:46–55) at evening prayer, and the Song of Simeon at night prayer (Luke 2:29–32) are ancient texts prayed since the beginning of the Christian faith and preserved in the New Testament.

This practice of praying at specific times throughout the day and night can be traced all the way back to daily worship in the Jewish Temple in Jerusalem, as well as to daily prayers in the synagogue. Christians continued the practice of daily prayers and incorporated it into their common life of faith in Christ. These five daily prayers of the Liturgical Hours are usually sung in monastic communities, but all Christians are invited and encouraged to use this resource to enrich their lives of faith and prayer, either together with others in parish churches or alone. The five hours are liturgical prayers, that is, official prayers of the Church. So even when a person prays them alone, she or he is in communion with the whole Church at prayer.

47. What's the difference then between Jewish prayer and Christian prayer?

Let's think for a moment about what they share in common. Like Christians, Jews bless and adore God. They also make prayers of petition and intercession, as well as of thanksgiving and praise.

Both Jews and Christians also treasure sacred scripture. For Jews the Hebrew Scriptures are God's Word, revealed through Moses and the prophets. The scriptures not only bring God's Word to us, they also provide us words and sentiments with which to respond to God, such as in the psalms and in other songs, prayers, and poems found throughout the Hebrew texts. Christians understand God's Word in the same way: as both revelation to us and a way for us to respond to the Holy One. The scriptures not only teach us about God, they also teach us how to lift our minds and hearts to God who has revealed the mystery of salvation to us.

The significant difference is Christian belief in Jesus as the Son of God. Jews, although they may honor Jesus as a prophet and a good man, do not pray to Jesus, only to the Father. Whereas the notion of God's Spirit is present throughout the Hebrew Bible, from Genesis (1:2) through the psalms (Ps 143:10) to the prophets (Ezek 11:24), the Holy Spirit as a third person of the Trinity is not part of Jewish belief.

48. Are there prayers in the New Testament?

Yes. The New Testament is filled with prayers of all types. Prayers used by the earliest Christian communities appear especially in the Gospel of Luke that contains Mary's song of praise (Luke 1:46–55), Zechariah's prophetic prayer about his son John the Baptist (Luke 1:68–79), the song of the angels at Jesus' birth (Luke 2:13–15), and Simeon's prayer in the temple (Luke 2:29–32).

Jesus himself prays often in the Gospels. He would have learned to pray from his parents at home, at synagogue (Luke 4:16), as well as in the Jerusalem Temple (Luke 2:41–52). He prays before important decisions such as choosing his disciples (Luke 6:12–16), and before significant events in his life such as the Transfiguration (Luke 9:28–36) and on the Mount of Olives the night before he died (Luke 22:39–46). As you can see from the scriptural citations, Luke's Gospel is especially full of references to and examples of early Christian prayer.

One unique aspect of Jesus' prayer is that he calls God *abba* (Mark 14:36), which in his native tongue of Aramaic was an intimate and endearing term for father, something like "daddy." Christians are invited by faith and the Holy Spirit also to pray to

God intimately as *abba* (Rom 8:15–16; Gal 4:6). John's Gospel provides us with the long prayer of intercession that Jesus offers on our behalf to his Father (John 17). This is often called Jesus' priestly prayer because he prays for us to God on the night before he offered his life for our salvation.

The New Testament, then, shapes the nature of Christian prayer, making it an intimate conversation with God in which we share with Jesus to whom we are united by the Holy Spirit.

49. Jesus taught his disciples to pray the Our Father, right?

Yes. The disciples once observed Jesus praying and, when he had finished, they asked him to teach them how to pray (Luke 11:1). Jesus responded with what has become known as the Lord's Prayer or the Our Father (Luke 11:2–4). A slightly longer and more familiar version of this prayer appears in Matthew's Gospel as part of Jesus' famous Sermon on the Mount (Matt 6:9–13).

The Lord's Prayer begins with the Christian's right, given us by Jesus, to address God intimately as Father, then moves into blessing or adoration ("hallowed—holy or blessed—be thy name"), and continues with petitions that God's kingdom of peace and justice be accomplished on Earth, that God's will be done in our lives, that we receive what we need ("our daily bread"), that we be forgiven as we forgive others, that we not succumb to temptation, and that we be delivered from all matter of evil.

50. Why do Protestants add the final phrase, "For thine is the kingdom, and the power, and the glory, forever and ever"?

Although this phrase does not appear as part of the Lord's Prayer in either Matthew or Luke's version, the early Christians soon added this final prayer of praise or doxology (from the Greek word for praise). It appears in Christian liturgies of the second century as part of the Lord's Prayer. In recognition of this ancient usage, it was restored to the Catholic Mass during the liturgical reforms of the Second Vatican Council. The assembly responds with this doxology immediately after the priest's declaration that we who have just prayed the Lord's Prayer, "wait in joyful hope" for his second coming.

51. During Mass can I pray using my own words or other prayers that I know?

For Catholics the Mass, or the Eucharistic Liturgy as it is also called, is the "summit and source" of all Christian faith and prayer.[17] Above all else it should be a time of deep personal prayer shared among the members of the faithful assembled for worship. The hymns, the official prayers led by the priest, the scripture readings and psalms, the homily and intercessions, the long Eucharistic Prayer over the gifts of bread and wine, and the reception of Holy Communion—all components of the Mass—are designed to lead people into a prayerful state of communion with Jesus and with each other through the Holy Spirit.

Personal prayers and devotions are very helpful in preparing our minds and hearts to celebrate Mass prayerfully. During the Mass itself, it is important to enter into the common prayers and hymns and to listen to the reading of God's Word. There may be times when personal devotions, even during Mass, can open us up to the grace that comes to us through the liturgy. Generally, however, it is better to let the liturgical prayers and readings inspire our minds and lift our hearts to God.

PART FOUR

Meditation and Contemplation

52. What is meditation?

Meditation is prayerful reflection in which we engage our mind and heart to focus on God or on some aspect of our faith. Meditation employs various capacities of the mind to concentrate on any experience considered in the light of faith in God: on a passage from scripture or other spiritual writing, on a scene from the life of Jesus or one of the saints, on a virtue such as hope or love or courage, or on a significant event in our own lives or in the lives of others. In meditating we use our memory, our imagination, and our capacity for reason and association for extended reflection on a particular idea or event.

53. So is meditation a kind of "holy thinking"?

It begins with thinking or reflecting on an idea or event in the light of faith. For example, reading Jesus' story of the prodigal son (Luke 15), we might put ourselves into the story as an observer, living at the house of this particular Jewish family two thousand years ago. Maybe we imagine ourselves to be the mother or sister (who are not mentioned in the text) or a servant of the household who knows the father and his two sons very well. Then we let the story play out as Jesus told it, but with our imaginative involvement. Such an exercise brings the story alive in new ways.

The next step in meditation moves from mind to heart. The exercise of our mind begins to stir our heart. We allow or foster feelings about the story, the characters in it, and our own affective reactions to their plight. We might feel sorrow for the prodigal son, perhaps associating him with a friend or a member of our own family who has lost his or her way and is alienated from everyone. We might feel the overwhelming joy of the father upon his son's return home. Or we might feel the confusion of the other "faith-

ful" son who never left home. These feelings then become part of
our prayer when we lift them up to God.

54. What if I'm meditating on an event from my own life?

The same pattern holds. We reflect on something that has happened to us by bringing it to God in prayer. We think carefully
about it in light of our faith and of God's loving concern for us. We
take responsibility for our actions and perhaps consider the conse-
quences of our choices. At some point we ask the Holy Spirit to stir
up within us feelings or affections that will pull us closer to God.

55. So feelings are part of meditation?

Yes. Think about how we share with a friend our thoughts
about an event from our own life or perhaps about a situation that
has affected us both. In such a conversation the exchange is not
only on the level of reason or discursive thought. We almost always
move from facts to feelings, from objective presentation of the
event to subjective feelings about the matter we are discussing. In
the same way when we meditate on a passage from scripture, on a
particular virtue, or on an event in our lives, we reflect on it in
God's presence, as we might with a sympathetic friend. We also
share our feelings about the topic, knowing that God responds
with infinite love and compassion.

56. So can I meditate on anything?

Yes, in the sense that we can bring anything to God in prayer.
There are many books by spiritual writers that offer suggestions
about topics for meditation, as well as about methods for practicing meditation. These books most often suggest as topics for meditation passages from scripture and other spiritual books; events
from the life of Jesus, Mary, or the saints; as well as significant events
in our personal lives. It is helpful to incorporate passages from

sacred scripture as a way to begin daily meditation. After a prayer-ful reading of scripture, we can move to a certain amount of time reflecting on the passage, integrating our own experience, allowing the Holy Spirit to open our minds and move our hearts.

57. You said "daily meditation." What's that about?

All the spiritual writers who have given advice or suggested methods for meditating recommend that it become a daily part of our life of faith. Meditation deepens our experience of God's abiding presence and greatly enriches our other prayers, both our private prayers as well as our participation in the liturgical prayers of the Church.

58. Who are some of these writers?

There are many. Since the Middle Ages explicit methods for meditation have appeared in Western Christian culture. You find meditation guides written by monks for monks such as the Carthusians and the Cistericans (also called Trappists). Meditations on the life of Christ were recommended by St. Bonaventure for his Franciscan brothers and sisters. In the sixteenth century new meth-ods for meditation were recommended by St. Ignatius of Loyola, founder of the Jesuits, in his famous *Spiritual Exercises*. St. Teresa of Avila also wrote many books such as *The Interior Castle* and *The Way of Perfection* for her Carmelite sisters. Her friend and fellow Carmelite, John of the Cross, wrote about the struggles of those who dedicated themselves to the daily practice of the spiritual life in his classic *Dark Night of the Soul*.

In the following centuries Francis de Sales and Alphonsus de Liguori built upon these classic spiritual writings to offer methods for meditation for their new religious communities. These new religious orders were engaged in active service of God's people and had to integrate daily meditation into their very busy pastoral lives. Their methods of meditation were designed for active priests, brothers, and sisters, instead of cloistered monks and nuns. As a result many lay people who wanted to pursue a more intense life of prayer began to read about and practice meditation as recommended by these saints.

59. Do I have to choose one of these methods if I want to meditate?

Not necessarily. It can be very helpful and instructive to read these authors and gain the advantage of their experience and their wisdom about prayer. You may decide to choose a particular method and stay with it. Or you may choose elements from various spiritual guides and integrate them into your own way of meditating.

All these methods can sometimes give the impression that meditation is a rather complicated and difficult affair. However, a closer look shows that they all share a basic pattern of preparing for meditation by choosing a topic or reading and asking God's guidance and grace, of engaging mind and heart in a variety of creative ways, and of moving from reflection and affection into conversation with God. After a while each person develops his or her own method, by adapting the advice of a spiritual writer, integrating meditation into the rhythms of one's own life, and following the promptings of the Holy Spirit.

60. Can I meditate just on scripture?

Certainly. Many people—priests, ministers, religious sisters and brothers, as well as laity—meditate each day on a passage from scripture. They might choose the readings for each day's Mass from the Lectionary, or they might follow some other way of selecting a text. This practice of meditating frequently on scripture, or on some other spiritual writing, using mind and heart and moving from reflection to conversation with God, is called *Lectio Divina* or Holy Reading. There are many books and aids that recommend ways to approach this practice.

61. What is contemplation?

Contemplation is a simple, quiet dwelling in the presence of God. Meditation, as we have seen, starts with a reading or event, moves to an exercise of mind and heart, and culminates in conversation with God. One way of understanding contemplation is to think of it as the step beyond conversation with God. As we approach the contemplative state, the mind begins to slow down and let go of the creative exercise that has enriched the practice of meditation. The heart ceases moving from one feeling to another and seeks to dwell in simple loving adoration of the Holy One. The words that have shaped our conversation with God fade into silent dwelling in the presence and power of God.

62. That sounds intense. Do many people practice contemplation?

It is intense. Spiritual writers who have experienced contemplation have used all kinds of analogies and language to describe it. The psalmist describes it as a weaned child with its mother (Ps 131:2). St. Paul writes about being lifted up to the "third heaven" in a kind of out-of-body experience (2 Cor 12:2). St. Augustine writes about a poignant, out-of-time moment of contemplation shared with his mother Monica shortly before her death.[18] Many mystics use the imagery of sexual love to try to capture the experience of God's presence during contemplation.[19]

The question of how many people experience contemplation is one only God could answer. Monks and nuns in all religious traditions dedicate their lives to meditation and contemplation. However, lay people are also called to prayer and many do practice daily meditation. Many devout believers in different religious traditions certainly do experience contemplation as part of their lives of prayer and dedication to God. Spiritual writers have often noted that even simple, everyday folk without knowledge of meditation techniques enjoy contemplative moments in their prayer, dwelling quietly and joyfully in God's presence.

63. What is a mystic?

A *mystic* is someone who experiences union with God through contemplation. In one sense any believer who experiences the presence of God and who abides in it lovingly, has a mystical experience. However, the term mystic usually refers to someone who has very powerful, recurring contemplative experiences of union with God, and who speaks or writes about that experience in an attempt to share it with others.

64. Who are some famous Christian mystics?

Paul the Apostle, John the Evangelist, Augustine of Hippo, Bernard of Clairvaux, Meister Eckhart, Hildegard of Bingen, Julian of Norwich, Catherine of Siena, Teresa of Avila, John of the Cross, George Fox (founder of the Quakers), Francis de Sales, Thérèse of Lisieux—the Little Flower—Dorothy Day, the list could go on and on. See the Further Resources chapter at the end of the book for more references.

65. Are there mystics in all religions?

All of the world's major religions have schools or sects that promote a certain practice of meditation that can lead to contemplation or mystical experience. Examples of mystical traditions in other religions include the Kabbalah and Hasidim in Judaism and Sufism in Islam. Many of the different yogas of Hinduism offer meditative ways and practices that lead to mystic contemplation.

In the Western Abrahamic religions of Judaism, Christianity, and Islam, mystical union with God is not understood to dissolve or annihilate the identity of the believer. The distinction between the creature and the Creator remains. The believer may have the experience of being temporarily "lost" in divine love during moments of ecstasy, but the theological basis of contemplation is the union of the human with the divine.

In Eastern religions, especially Hinduism, mysticism involves the dissolution or return of the individual soul *(atman)* into the all-encompassing reality of the Godhead *(Brahman)* from which any soul is only temporarily and superficially distinct while in this life. The distinction between creature and Creator ultimately collapses back into the original unity of the Godhead. Mysticism is a fore-taste of this final condition of undifferentiated oneness.

This, at least, is a theological distinction between Western and Eastern mysticism. In practice Western mystics describe moments of "losing oneself completely" in the divine, and even of "ceasing to exist" *(fana* in the Arabic texts of Islamic mystics). Conversely, Eastern mystics, especially those who follow the *bhakti* yoga of Hinduism, speak of their intense exchange of love with God.

66. How would I start to meditate?

The best first step is probably to talk to a priest, pastor, or spiritual director who could introduce you to some of the books and articles on meditation. It's also helpful to work with a spiritual director, guide, or mentor who could teach or coach you in the practice of meditation—either in a particular way such as the *Spiritual Exercises* of St. Ignatius or the Centering Prayer of the Cistercians—or who could help you find your own method and practice.

67. What's Centering Prayer?

Centering Prayer is a path to contemplation, but one that is somewhat different from meditation as we described it. Centering Prayer as it is known today was made popular by the Cistercian Monks of St. Joseph's Abbey in Spencer, Massachusetts. However, it has ancient roots in the early centuries of the Church, especially in the writings of St. John Cassian (360–435 CE).

John brought the spiritual practices of the desert monks and nuns of the Eastern churches to the Western Church. Among these practices was the Jesus Prayer that involves repeating the name

"Jesus" or the phrase "Lord, have mercy" or the prayer "Lord Jesus Christ, Son of God, have mercy on me, a sinner." The nature of this practice is to repeat one of these prayers, either vocally or silently, for extensive periods of time, perhaps with the aid of a rosary. This Christian mantra slowly pushes all other thoughts, concerns, and feelings aside so that one's mind and heart is empty of all else but God.

In the fourteenth century an unknown English author wrote a book on prayer called *The Cloud of Unknowing.* This book elaborates on the Jesus Prayer tradition and offers practical advice on how to empty one's mind of all distractions, using a mantra or prayer word. The Cistercian monks of St. Joseph's took this practice, combined it with some simple breathing techniques from Eastern meditative practice as well as with insights from depth psychology, in order to offer contemporary Christians the richness of this ancient practice.

The twentieth-century British Benedictine monk John Main developed and taught a meditative practice similar to Centering Prayer which he called simply Christian Meditation. It remains a popular practice among Christians of many denominations who find their participation in this "monastery without walls" to be an essential part of their life of faith and prayer.

68. So these special kinds of prayer are not reserved for priests or monks and nuns?

St. Paul affirms that every Christian is united with the risen Lord Jesus in ways that affect the very core of our being. He recommends what we call contemplation as a part of Christian life for all believers: "I pray that you may have the power to comprehend, with all the saints, what is the breadth and length and height and depth, and to know the love of Christ that surpasses knowledge, so that you may be filled with all the fullness of God" (Eph 3:18–19). Similarly, St. John writes in ways that describe every Christian as a potential mystic. On the night before he dies, Jesus speaks to his Father about his disciples—about us: "The glory that you have given me I have given them, so that they may be one, as we are one, I in them and you in me, that they may become completely one, so that the world may know that you have sent me and have loved them even as you have loved me" (John 17:22–23).

Prayer is part of every Christian's journey of faith. Meditation and contemplation are ways to enrich our experience of prayer and to extend—in the words of St. Paul—the breadth, length, height, and depth of our praying. If we incorporate some kind of regular meditation, contemplation, or Centering Prayer into our life of faith, that practice will enrich our other prayers, both our personal, private prayers as well as our participation in the liturgical or formal prayers of the Church.

69. Will God help me if I decide to start meditating?

All forms of prayer—from a child's "Now I lay me down to sleep…" to a simple recitation of the Our Father to the heights of contemplation—are responses to God's revelation of divine love in Jesus. Just as God first speaks to us, so God also helps us in our response. Grace suffuses our every prayer. The Holy Spirit guides us, prompts us, and assists us in our journey of faith and in our lives of prayer: "Likewise the Spirit helps us in our weakness; for we do not know how to pray as we ought, but that very Spirit intercedes with sighs too deep for words. And God, who searches the heart, knows what is the mind of the Spirit" (Rom 8: 26–27).

So the Spirit will lead us in our meditation and contemplation, both during times of joy and consolation as well as during times when we are distracted, disturbed, or even distressed by our lack of fervor or interest. God rushes to meet us in prayer. God is always waiting, like the expectant father of the prodigal son, scanning the horizons of our lives for the first sign of our approach in prayer, longing to greet us, embrace us, and celebrate our return with prodigious, divine joy.

PART FIVE

Prayer in Other Traditions

70. How long has prayer been around?

Anthropologists have found evidence of prayer even among Neanderthals. Their burial sites indicate belief in an afterlife and funereal rituals that suggest prayer for the well-being of the deceased. Our own ancestors, early homo sapiens, left traces in the cave art of the Paleolithic era that point to symbolic, magical rites that surely included prayers to a powerful spirit for success in the hunt, and perhaps for thanksgiving afterward.

At the very dawn of literature, the first written record of prayer is found in the *Epic of Gilgamesh* from ancient Babylon (modern Iraq) around 2750 BCE. Toward the beginning of this ancient tale, preserved on tablets in cuneiform writing, women of the city of Uruk pray to the goddess Ishtar that they be freed from tyranny and abuse by an enemy king who has enslaved them. Their prayers augur countless such requests for rescue, raised to God by exiles and victims throughout the ages.

Prayers fill the classical texts of Homer, cover the temple walls of tribal religions, and imbue the myths of all cultures. Prayer has always been and still remains at the very heart of culture.

71. What are some of the oldest prayers still in use?

The most ancient prayers of humankind still in use are preserved in the Hindu scriptures called the Vedas. These are the meditations and teachings of saints, mystics, and seers from the Indian subcontinent. The oldest written Veda comes from around 1500 BCE and contains a prayer to accompany a ritual sacrifice by fire. There are thousands of Vedic prayers used today among the many sects and devotions of Hinduism.

The *Upanishads* are sections of the Vedas devoted to meditation on the nature of the Holy One or *Brahman*. These ancient prayerful reflections and mystical revelations have inspired many in both East and West.

72. How do Hindus pray?

In many different ways. Hinduism is a vast religion with an immense collection of myths and sacred scriptures, lavish art, elaborate rituals, and an almost infinite variety of gods and goddesses or *avatars*. These are specific and local revelations or incarnations of the Infinite Godhead.

Hindu prayer comprises popular devotions to major divinities such as Kali or Krishnu, as well as ritual sacrifices to the local deities or avatars of one's village or hometown (not unlike Catholic devotions to local saints). The rituals of worship and devotion are called *puja*. They often involve ceremonial washings and can be done alone or with others, in silence or with vocal prayer. Christians who visit a Hindu temple are usually struck by the combination of ritual practice, informal familiarity, and a general joyful atmosphere.

Hindus also worship at home by creating a shrine with statues or other representations of the individual's chosen form of God. They may practice *pujas* at home by offering flowers, water, or food as sacrificial prayer. Readings from the Vedas and *Upanishads,* incense, candles, bells, litanies, and mantras all enrich the experience of worship. Hinduism also contains the three daily prayers or *sandhyas* practiced by the observant.

73. What are the *sandhyas*?

Sandhya means "junction" and these are prayers at the three junctions of the day: night to morning, forenoon to afternoon, and evening to night. At each *sandhya* the devotee prays the sacred *Gayatri* mantra that comes from the ancient Vedas. The repetition of this short prayer is a petition to the Divine One to awaken mind and soul, and to bring the one who prays into union with *Brahman*.

74. Do Hindus practice meditation and contemplation?

One of the great gifts of Hinduism to the world is its tradition of yoga. Yoga is an ancient Sanskrit word that refers to the practice of a discipline that leads to union with God. Today we usually think of yoga as a set of exercises and controlled breathing that improves physical health and emotional well-being. The practice of *hatha* yoga, as this is known, can certainly provide many benefits. However, this type of yoga is only part of the much wider yogic tradition.

Yoga is primarily ancient Hindu teachings on how daily meditation, supported and strengthened by carefully practiced bodily positions and gestures, can lead the practitioner to an experience of the presence of the divine within. Beneath the many different kinds of yoga is the basic Hindu belief that every human soul *(atman)* emerges from and returns to the Godhead *(Brahman).* Yoga is disciplined prayer that leads one into the mystery of *atman-Brahman.*

75. Can Christians use yoga in their praying?

Yes. Yoga represents the collective wisdom from millennia of reflection and experience on the nature and practice of prayer. As St. Paul advises, "test everything; hold fast to what is good" (1 Thess 5:21; see also Phil 4:8). For some Christians the prayerful disciplines of yoga greatly assist in raising their mind and heart to God.

Combining Hindu yoga with the Christian prayer requires some attention to both similarities and difference in belief. Christians believe that Jesus is the fullness of the revelation of God, and that in Christ, the Divine Word, all creation originates and is ultimately reunited with God (Col 1:15–20; Eph 1:9–11). Christians also believe that each human soul is uniquely loved and embraced by God. A Christian can use the wisdom of Hindu yogic practices to enter more deeply into the mystery of Christ, even while learning to appreciate how Hindus approach their experience of the Holy One. The contemporary Paulist priest Thomas Ryan has dedicated his ministry to helping Christians appreciate and integrate the practical wisdom of yoga in their lives of faith and prayer.

76. What are Buddhist prayers like?

Midway through the first millennium BCE (around 800–500 BCE), amid social upheaval and change on the Indian subcontinent, a religious revival produced a new emphasis on prayer and the pursuit of holiness. This was the origin of Buddhism and Jainism, both reformations of ancient Hindu tradition.

Like Hinduism, Buddhism is not one, well-defined religious tradition and practice. There are varieties of Buddhist teachings, traditions, rituals, and practices found in various forms throughout the world, especially in the East. Buddhism rejected the ancient Vedic rituals and social castes of Hinduism, and invited all who might listen to the teachings of the Buddha to experience enlightenment or *bodhi*. Various forms of contemporary Buddhist meditation or simply practice, as it is called, together with a life of moderation and morality, promise to bring the devotee to enlightenment. The purer forms of Buddhist prayer are designed to empty the mind of thought and release the heart of feeling so that one can transcend the limits of the self and enter into the greater life cycle of being and nonbeing.

The goal of Buddhist practice is to free one from suffering *(dukkha)* and from desire or attachment *(tanha)*, which is the cause of suffering. The result of this freedom is the unbridled happiness of enlightenment. Buddhist practice, therefore, emphasizes freedom from whatever causes suffering and sorrow. Hindu yoga as well as Christian spirituality emphasizes freedom for union with the Holy One who is the source of all happiness and joy. For Christians Christ is the Way to communion with God.

77. What is a prayer wheel?

Prayer wheels are found especially in the Tibetan Buddhist tradition. They can be made of metal, wood, or leather and are hung on a spindle that allows them to be easily spun or rotated. Sacred mantras are written on the outside of the wheel surface. The devotee spins the wheel while slowly and prayerfully repeating the mantra written on the prayer wheel. Each rotation of the wheel is equivalent to a repetition of the mantra, beneficial to the one who prays and to the surroundings.

While we're on this subject, in the Himalayas one also finds prayer flags blowing in the wind. Indigenous Tibetan culture seems to be the origin of prayer flags, even predating Buddhism there. These colorful, rectangular flags represent different aspects of Buddhist teaching and bless the mountains they adorn.

78. So can Christians use Buddhist prayer and meditation?

Christians may find Buddhist practice to be helpful along their journey of faith. The famous American Trappist monk Thomas Merton studied Buddhist practice and was deeply interested in the work of the Dalai Lama, the Vietnamese Buddhist monk Thich Nhat Hanh, and other Buddhist scholars and monks. In Buddhist psychology he found many insights into the human experience of prayer, transcendence, and the mystery of God.

Christians can study Buddhist practice and adapt it to their own spiritual lives in ways that enrich their faith. The noticeable silence of Buddhist teaching on the nature or existence of God stands in stark contract to the Christian affirmation of God's love revealed in Christ. However, Buddhist reluctance and reticence regarding the Holy can serve as a reminder that all language about and symbols of God fall infinitely short of the realities to which they point.

79. It seems that prayer is important to Muslims. Is that right?

All Muslims are called to "be steadfast in prayer" (Qur'an II,3). This injunction at the very beginning of the Qur'an is lived out in the *Salat,* the five daily prayers that every devout Muslim observes. Every day, just before dawn, at noon, in late afternoon, just after sunset, and before retiring, a muezzin proclaims the *adhan,* the call to "Come to Prayer," reminding all believers that God is Great and worthy of worship.

Believers respond by performing the ablutions or ritual washings, spreading out their prayer carpets, and turning toward Mecca—there are many traditional and contemporary ways to determine the proper direction or *qibla.* The *Salat* itself is a complex sequence of bows, prostrations, and prayers that pull the whole believer, body and soul, into submission before God. The frequency and intensity of *Salat* make daily prayer the very heart of Muslim religion.

80. Do Muslims pray to Jesus?

Although the Qur'an is the sacred book for Muslims, they also revere the Bible and they honor Jesus as a great prophet. They also honor Mary his mother, whom they call Miriam. However, they do not believe that Jesus is the divine Son of God, nor do they believe in the Trinity, which they judge to be a form of polytheism. So, no, they do not pray to Jesus nor to the Holy Spirit.

81. What is Ramadan?

Ramadan is observed during the ninth month of the Islamic calendar as a time of fasting (from sunrise to sunset), of intensified prayer, and of attention to works of charity. Like the five daily prayers, the annual observance of Ramadan brings the importance of prayer to the forefront of every Muslim's life.

82. Don't Muslims make a pilgrimage to Mecca?

The *Hajj* is a responsibility of all Muslims who enjoy the health and money to make this once-in-a-lifetime pilgrimage to Mecca during the twelfth month of the Islamic calendar. Like Christian pilgrimages, it is a journey inspired by faith and accomplished in a prayerful spirit. The *Hajj* climaxes in the prayerful circling of the Ka'ba, the sacred shrine in the center of the great mosque of Mecca.

83. Can Christians use Muslim prayers?

Many Christians have been deeply moved by the intensity of Islamic prayer and fasting and by the ways in which it envelops the life of a devout Muslim believer. However, the daily performance of *Salat* as well as the observance of Ramadan are so explicit and exact as to require long practice and deep appreciation before they could be integrated into the prayer life of a believing Christian. One must also respect the sensibilities of some Muslims who may not understand the adoption of their culturally specific prayer forms by those outside Islam. Non-Muslims, for example, may not participate in the *Hajj* because only Muslims are allowed in Mecca.

In addition, there are theological differences that must be taken into account. Both the Call to Prayer and the five daily prayers proclaim the Islamic testimony that Muhammad is God's prophet. A Qur'anic passage repeated throughout *Salat* proclaims of God that "He begetteth not, Nor is He begotten" (Qur'an CXII, 3). Christian prayer arises out of belief in the nature of Jesus as God's "only begotten Son" and of the finality and fullness of God's self revelation through Jesus.

On the other hand the Qur'an as well as many other Islamic writings, especially those of the mystical Sufis, can enrich the spiritual lives of Christians who seek to explore how others listen and respond to God. Certainly Christians and Muslims can pray together, both joining in prayers written to suit an interfaith gathering, as well as respectfully observing each other's distinctive prayer forms.

84. Can people from all these different faiths actually pray together?

Pope John Paul II thought so. In a famous event in the history of religions, he invited leaders of all the world's major religions and sects to a common prayer for peace in Assisi, Italy, on October 27, 1986. Everyone prayed in their own way and in silence for peace in the world, standing side by side in the great basilica that houses the Porziuncola or little chapel once restored by St. Francis.[20]

John Paul was criticized by some Catholics and other Christians for compromising in this shared prayer the uniqueness of faith in Jesus Christ as the one Lord and Savior. Of course, the pope was in no way conceding this most fundamental of Christian doctrines. However, he was respecting the religious path and spiritual identity of others, and emphasizing the importance of mutual respect and understanding if we are to build a worldwide culture of peace and dignity.

Catholics and other Christians can likewise, from time to time, pray with those from other faiths, knowing that whatever our different traditions and teachings, there is one God who cherishes all alike. The Second Vatican Council called Roman Catholics and all Christians to engage in dialogue and collaboration with the followers of other religions, and, while remaining faithful to Christ, to "recognize, preserve and promote the good things, spiritual and moral" that are found among other religions.[21]

PART SIX

Struggling to Pray

85. Can I pray if I have doubts about my faith and even about God?

Certainly. All believers have doubts about religious faith at some time in their lives. We may even question the existence of God. Our religious journeys lead through many different landscapes, from high trails of faith rising toward clear certainty, to foggy bogs of doubt leaving us lost and disoriented. Theologian Paul Tillich wrote that doubt is "an intrinsic element in faith."[22] Doubt is not the opposite of faith. It is its complement. Like the New Testament Christian who prayed to Jesus: "I believe; help my unbelief" (Mark 9:24), we, too, can bring our doubt to prayer.

Faith is not only the content of religious doctrine that a believer accepts and affirms (e.g., Christian faith in Jesus as risen Lord and Savior); it is also a discrete way, a distinctive manner of knowing. It is different from knowledge that is based solely on the syllogisms of reason or the empirical proofs of science. It is a way of receiving the events of our lives and an approach to understanding the course of human history that affirms the possibility of their inherent meaning and purpose. It is a rational manner of knowing that remains profoundly open to and expectant of divine revelation in the very process of perceiving and interpreting the particulars of our experience.

By its very nature, then, faith invites doubt because of its arresting attentiveness to the unexpected, its willingness to entertain transcendence, its presupposition that human reason functions best when it suspects its own limits. Every prayer we offer is an act of faith. Every prayer is thereby also an occasion for doubt, that is, an exercise of radical openness to received meaning that is not of our own making. So, yes, we can pray if we have doubts.

86. Can an agnostic pray?

An *agnostic* is a person who believes that questions about ultimate matters must be answered with "we just don't know" (which
is the meaning of the Greek *a-gnosis*). Whereas the believer inte-
grates faith and doubt into a life of commitment, the agnostic nur-
tures doubt and refrains from religious commitment. As John
Henry Newman wrote, when it comes to questions of faith, nei-
ther believer nor agnostic can have certainty, that is, absolute
proven knowledge beyond any doubt. The believer, however, has
enough certitude to make a commitment in faith and love, despite
doubt.

In one sense the very definition of prayer that we have used
throughout this book leads to the conclusion that an agnostic
would not pray. However, an agnostic might raise mind and heart
tentatively, with some faint hope that there could be a divine listener. An agnostic might cast a furtive glance heavenward while
seeking good things for others and for the world. However, the
nature of such provisional prayers is very different from the fervent
pleas of a believer, even one with significant doubts. The difference
lies in the believer's personal commitment to the Holy One.

Agnosticism can be a permanent life choice. It can also be
part of a longer, more complex journey of spiritual search and
questioning. So in answering the question of whether or not an
agnostic can pray, we need to respect each person's history and dignity, and to remember that categories like "believer" and "agnostic" do not capture the fullness of any person's life or identity.

87. What about an atheist?

An *atheist* is someone who has answered the question of
God's existence in the negative: there is no god (the meaning of
the Greek *a-theos*). Like a believer, an atheist may occasionally
doubt the certainty of his or her conviction that God does not
exist. However, the atheist chooses to affirm the lack of any tran-
scendent meaning or destiny in the universe. Usually this convic-

tion rests upon the persuasiveness of reason and the power of empirical proof. Belief in God for which there is no discernible evidence seems unreasonable or even irrational.

So an atheist would have little interest in the very personal act of faith that we call prayer. However, we should repeat the caveat at the end of the previous question. Philosophical terms and religious categories do not capture the fullness nor the essence of any individual. Atheism may be a lifelong choice. It may also be one part of a person's pilgrimage through this life.

88. Can I pray if I am angry with God?

A quick search shows that the noun *anger* appears twenty-nine times and the adjective *angry* eleven times in the great Hebrew prayers known as the psalms. In almost every instance the reference is to God's anger with the Jews or with those who harm the Jews: "Will you be angry with us forever? Will you prolong your anger to all generations?" (Ps 85:5). The Jews even prayed (with some anger in their voice, one suspects) that God exercise his anger against their enemies: "Pour out your indignation upon them; and let your burning anger overtake them" (Ps 69:24). God's anger is also a recurring theme in the story of Job, who himself gets angry with his three friends when they constantly try to rational-ize his suffering.

In the New Testament Jesus shows his anger with the buyers and sellers who profane the Jerusalem Temple: "My house shall be called a house of prayer" (Matt 21:13; Mark 11:17; Luke 19:46). He also got angry with those who preferred legal observance to human compassion (Mark 3:5; John 7:23). His parables are often stories about people who themselves were angry (Matt 18:34; Luke 14:21; 15:28).

The Jews were comfortable with the notion of God's righteous anger and were not afraid to refer to it in their prayers. Jesus, who spoke often of God's love, also expressed his own anger at times. Anger is a normal part of our lives, and biblical images of God portray anger as a divine sentiment as well. We can bring our anger to prayer. We can lift it up to God along with the other thoughts and sentiments that fill and overflow our mind and heart. Anger is a normal response to loss, to the violation of human rights, to injustice—themes that run throughout the psalms. Righteous anger can even move us to prayer, just as it can move us to take action in order to make wrongs right.

However, there may also be times when we ask God to deliver us from anger, from the temptation to remain in our rage and nurse our resentment over something that has happened to us. When anger persists without resolution, when we wall up ourselves in the eye of the storm of our own fury, when we develop a lifestyle of calculated antagonism or bitterness, then anger can get in the way of our prayer. It can weigh down mind and heart, preventing us from lifting them up to God. Some people's chronic anger gets fixated on God. Their anger fractures their relationship with God whom they hold responsible for whatever ill or evil has befallen them. In such cases anger can become a barrier to prayer.

Anger erupts in so many verses of scripture because it is such a normal and pervasive part of life. Scripture is the story of God's involvement in human life and history. Anger invades our prayer for the same reasons. Anger will be a factor sooner or later in all our relationships with family and friends. We can expect it will also eventually be part of our relationship with God. Our goal should not be to avoid anger in our spiritual lives, but rather to be prudent and judicious in what we do with it.

89. Can I pray that something bad will happen to evildoers?

As mentioned, there are passages in scripture where the psalmist's anger at what has happened to God's people erupts into a prayer for vengeance. A startling example is in Psalm 137: Jerusalem and the Temple have been destroyed, thousands of Jews brutally murdered, and the rest sent into exile in Babylon. This psalm expresses the great sorrow and loss of the exiles, and ends with a request that God bless with happiness whoever kills the infant children of the Babylonians by dashing them against rocks (Ps 137:9). Strong language!

In contrast Jesus teaches in the Sermon on the Mount: "You have heard that it was said, 'You shall love your neighbor and hate your enemy.' But I say to you, Love your enemies and pray for those who persecute you, so that you may be children of your Father in heaven; for he makes his sun to rise on the evil and on the good, and sends rain on the righteous and on the unrighteous" (Matt 5:43–45). St. Paul advises, "Beloved, never avenge yourselves, but leave room for the wrath of God; for it is written, 'Vengeance is mine, I will repay, says the Lord'" (Rom 12:19). On the contrary: "If your enemies are hungry, feed them; if they are thirsty, give them something to drink; for by doing this you will heap burning coals on their heads" (Rom 12:20).

Although we can express our anger in prayer, and honestly integrate our feelings into conversation with God, we also pray in the Our Father that we be forgiven as we forgive those who have harmed us. Prayer becomes an occasion to move, by God's grace and in good time, beyond resentment and vengeance toward forgiveness and reconciliation.

90. What if someone is so ill—physically or mentally—that they can't concentrate long or well enough to pray?

In his last book, *The Gift of Peace,* Cardinal Bernadin of Chicago wrote that the hardest part about his illness was that the pain was sometimes so great he could not even pray. Severe physical pain, high fever, anxiety, and depression can make it difficult if not impossible to pray in the ways we ordinarily do.

We spoke earlier (question 29) about sacrifice as a prayerful offering to God that symbolizes our desire to raise mind and heart to God. When we are in such physical or mental pain that we cannot concentrate on God or gain access to the center of our being, we can simply offer our pain itself as a sacrificial prayer to God, and God, who knows all things, will receive it "as an evening sacrifice" of praise (Ps 141:2).

91. What about the mentally disabled?

Children who may be impaired by various mental disabilities can be brought into the life of prayer that sustains their families or the communities of faith into which they were born. Parents can slowly introduce them to prayer and teach them to pray as they are able. Our simple definition of prayer as the lifting of mind and heart to God, or asking God for good things, can be helpful here. Children with congenital mental disabilities can be tutored in lifting mind and heart to God in and through the minds and hearts of their parents and caregivers who invite them into loving interaction and joyful stimulation.

The Christian teaching of the body of Christ is pertinent here. All Christian prayer is through, with, and in Christ to God the Father in union with the Holy Spirit. All members of the Christian community are united as adopted daughters and sons of God (Eph 1:5). Members of the Church whose mental or emotional capacity might be in some ways limited or impaired are no less adopted and embraced by God, even if they may not come to "know" God in ways that others do (remembering that no person's "knowledge" of God can begin to capture the reality of the Infinite Holy One). Children with congenital conditions, as well as adults who have suffered brain injury, share with all members of the body of Christ in the love and mercy of God.

As we have already noted, many persons devote considerable time and effort to developing a life of prayer, and even to a disciplined practice of careful meditation and contemplation. However, the prayer of the pope, of the Dalai Lama, or of a holy mystic is no more or less precious to the Infinite Holy One than the simple, halting prayers of a child in the arms of its mother or father.

92. Can people who suffer from Alzheimer's disease pray?

The great psychological pain of Alzheimer's disease is the gradual loss of memory and the alterations in personality that ensue. Both patient and loved ones suffer from this deterioration. With drastic loss of memory comes a slow loss of self, for our sense of self is knit together by the intricate patterns of memory and connection that have been woven throughout our lives. Those who have lost a loved one to Alzheimer's disease will tell you that they lost the person long before she or he physically died.

For those who care for and about a patient with Alzheimer's, it is important to remember that God does not forget. All the events and experiences of the patient's life that may slowly fade from awareness and seem to disintegrate with the failing brain, including one's knowledge of and relationship with God, are kept in every detail in the infinite, unfailing mind and heart of God who never forgets (Isa 49:15). Those who love the patient can constantly offer his or her life to God as a loving sacrifice that God will receive, accept, and transform.

In this sense, then, although painful, it does not matter that Alzheimer's patients slowly lose the capacity to pray as they once did. The prayers of their loved ones, the universal prayer of the Church, and the prayer of the Holy Spirit (Rom 8:26–27) all supply in infinite abundance for their relationship with God from whom nothing, not even the devastation of Alzheimer's disease, can separate them (Rom 8:38–39).

93. Can alcoholics or drug addicts pray?

Addiction is a complex condition with interacting physical, psychological, social, and spiritual components. In itself, addiction does not preclude a person from relationship with God and cannot prevent the power of divine grace from reaching the addict. Once they have begun to admit, accept, and deal with their addiction, many people will testify that God's grace made their journey back to wholeness possible.

However, while a person is in the throes of addiction, be it to a substance or a lifestyle, his or her capacity to be present to others is greatly limited. The addict lives for and is obsessed by whatever it is that seems to fill the huge black hole in the center of the soul. Mind and heart are continuously distracted. Conversation with God is as hampered as conversation with anyone else. Prayer is not impossible for an addict, but the very nature of addiction highlights the role of God's grace in such straits.

For many people their healing from addiction includes a spiritual component. The addict's experience of return to the fullness of life so often involves a realization of God's abiding presence— God who was, is, and always will be within and around us. Recovery is discovery of God's endless initiatives of love in one's life. Recovery, then, involves prayer as one's response to grace, to God's infinite offers of love.

PART SEVEN

Committing to Prayer

94. What do you mean by "committing to prayer"?

Prayer is an expression of our relationship with God. That relationship may be occasional: God becomes part of our lives when we are in trouble because of our own behavior, or when we suffer the effects of what others have done to us. So we turn to God in prayer for help, asking for relief and redress. Sometimes we relate to the people in our lives in a similar way, contacting them when needed for the help they can give us. There is nothing necessarily wrong with an occasional outreach for help to another, be it to God, an old friend, or a member of our own family. But the limited extent of the relationship is usually clear to those on both sides.

Or our relationship with God may be more conventional. We meet God at prearranged times and places as we do with family and friends (e.g., Sunday visits to our grandparents that were an important part of our youth or the Saturday morning coffee klatch with friends). So once a week we pray, perhaps alone, perhaps together with an assembly of believers. Here again, there is nothing wrong with such an arrangement. The weekly visits—with God or with family and friends—can be a very important part of our lives filling the rest of the week with meaning, purpose, and expectation.

Committing to prayer means working it into our lives in some regular way. Weekly worship can be a good place to start. Or perhaps as part of our daily routine we pray just before we retire or we may decide to pray every morning before we begin the day's business. Committing to prayer involves making space in our lives, taking time from other responsibilities, and setting aside all for visiting with God.

To commit to pray, each in our own way, is to move beyond occasion or convenience in our spiritual lives and begin a journey. That journey will change us and our lives. There will be times when we will get tired along the way, and our commitment will wane. There will other times when our prayer will invigorate us so that we stride along with confidence. And there will come times when we completely lose our way and wonder why we ever began in the first place. Like any relationship, commitment to prayer must sustain itself through difficult times. Like any journey, a life of regular prayer leads us through rough places as well as smooth.

There is a difference between occasional prayer prompted by need or convention and prayer that is part of a committed relationship with God. It is not a difference of moral superiority or spiritual supremacy. It is the difference that commitment makes to any relationship—a difference of experience, insight, familiarity, expectation, and hope. Regular prayer changes a person's life, just as commitment in a relationship makes all the difference.

95. What if I haven't prayed for a very long time? How do I get started?

Keep it short and simple. A complicated formula or arrangement can quickly become difficult to sustain. Choose a simple prayer with which to begin or end the day and stick to it. Take a few moments throughout the day just to remember God's presence by finding a quiet place. Some people will take a particular verse of scripture and repeat it several times during the day. Others will use simple phrases like "Lord Jesus, have mercy on me" or "I give you thanks and praise, O Lord" at certain times.

After a while you will notice gentle promptings to do more of the same or to move to different prayers, such as the psalms or particular devotions to the Virgin Mary or the saints. These are moments of God's grace guiding us slowly into deeper currents of prayer that will gradually move us along our spiritual voyage. In our conversations with other people, we look for cues and listen for leads that direct our responses and steer the exchange in one direction or another. During prayer we are in conversation with

God. God will guide and move and direct us. We need only to remain open and expectant.

96. If I am living an immoral life, can I still pray?

Certainly. God's grace is available to all. In fact, God shows preference for the "lost": "What do you think? If a shepherd has a hundred sheep, and one of them has gone astray, does he not leave the ninety-nine on the mountains and go in search of the one that went astray? And if he finds it, truly I tell you, he rejoices over it more than over the ninety-nine that never went astray" (Matt 18:11–13).

Prayer is not so much the dutiful path back to God from a life of sin. God, it seems, has already covered that route by blazing a trail to find and embrace and lift the sinner up onto the strong divine shoulders. Prayer is the sinner's joyful response. So the fact that you even ask this question is in itself evidence that God has already met you just where you are. Prayer is your thank you and a request that this same God carry you back to where you belong.

97. Does it help to talk to someone confidentially about prayer?

Yes, especially if you feel the need to do so. Although prayer is a very personal experience, in most religious traditions faith is not a private matter. Certainly in Judaism, Christianity, and Islam the role of the faith community is central to religious experience. We are called to support each other in our lives of faith, hope, and love: "Let the word of Christ dwell in you richly; teach and admonish one another in all wisdom; and with gratitude in your hearts sing psalms, hymns, and spiritual songs to God" (Col 3:16).

We can learn from those members of our faith community who have devoted themselves to a life of prayer. Some priests, pastors, and other ministers, lay and ordained, have studied the theology and practice of prayer. They can be great resources for others who want to learn more about prayer and who might need help in interpreting their own experience of prayer. If you find yourself being drawn deeper into a life of prayer, a spiritual director may be of great help.

98. What is a spiritual director?

A *spiritual director* is someone who accompanies us on our spiritual journey, helping us along the pilgrimage of prayer and faith. A spiritual director is someone who has studied theology, who is dedicated to his or her own life of prayer, and who has received some training in the art of helping others discover and express the sacred dimension in their life stories. They may be a priest or religious or lay person. Although spiritual direction has long been part of the Catholic tradition, it is also increasingly common among Protestants.

Spiritual directors are not psychological or pastoral counselors trained to guide clients grow through and out of behavioral and emotional problems. The focus of spiritual direction is to help others respond to the presence and power of God in the events of life and in the depths of the soul. The local priest or pastor can help you find a spiritual director. There are also Web sites with helpful information mentioned among the Further Resources chapter at the end of this book.

99. If I pray every day, won't prayer become just a habit?

Well, yes. But let's take a moment to consider what a habit is. As we regularly repeat a certain action or behavior, we grow accustomed to it and develop an aptitude for it. What once may have been difficult, requiring a lot of concentration or attention, has become more a part of who we are and how we act. We all have both good habits and bad habits, and so much of our daily life is shaped and directed by the habits of thinking, feeling, and choosing that we have developed through conscious effort and regular practice.

Let's consider the habit of running. If we want to make physical exercise a regular part of our lives, then we have to work it into our daily or weekly schedules. At first all the things necessary for running require some forethought and planning, such as choosing a time and a route, stretching before and after our run, selecting music to listen to as we run, having the right running shoes and apparel, checking the temperature, and making sure we don't eat too soon before or afterward. Little by little, if we stick to our commitment, all these details require less concentration, preparation, and energy. They become second nature to us. We do them almost without thinking. We've developed the habit of exercise. All the various details needed to make running a regular part of our lives have become habitual to us. We enjoy all the benefits of the exercise with minimum need for processing and preparing the necessary components.

In similar ways prayer can become a good habit. All the details that help us pray—such as choosing a time and place, making sure the cell phone is off, calming and quieting our minds and hearts and bodies, making the intention to pray, selecting a passage from scripture or other text for meditation, practicing a posture that helps us enter prayer more easily—become a natural part of who we are and how we live. Prayer becomes second nature to us, integrated into how we live our days and nights, how we think and feel, how we consider decisions and make choices. The habit of prayer develops into the virtue of prayer, that is, it becomes a vital part of our character and of our nature.

God's grace is an essential part of prayer. Our initial steps toward prayer are a response to God's love for us. Grace gradually guides and shapes all the components of our prayer and helps us weave it into the fabric of our daily lives. Even after prayer becomes habitual, grace courses through all the aspects of our praying. Grace constantly inclines our minds and turns our hearts to God's power and presence. Grace sustains us when prayer, despite its being a habit and a virtue, becomes difficult and burdensome. If and when prayer becomes so habitual as to be taken for granted, then grace startles us with new insight and unimagined perspectives that take us further along the pilgrimage that is prayer.

100. If I stay at it, will my prayer life change as I age?

Definitely. Prayer is the lifting of mind and heart to God and asking good things of God. As we travel through life, our minds and our hearts change. We constantly learn new things that reshape our ways of thinking and alter our perspectives. Our hearts also change as we enjoy life's good things and suffer its sorrows. Advancing in age and experience, we assess our needs in different ways. Our priorities shift and our concerns adjust to life circumstances. As we age, what we lift up to or ask of God can change significantly.

It is not only the content of our prayer that changes as we grow older; the way we pray also changes. Let's take the example of a young married couple. The things they discuss, the concerns they share, what they ask of each other will change as they age together, perhaps raise a family, and struggle to support each other and survive in the world. The concerns of a couple married for five years are very different thirty years later.

However, something else changes as well. With long and loving commitment, the very manner of their communication itself grows and develops. What once took several minutes to explain, now takes just a word or two. What at the beginning required words at all, now needs only a glance or quiet gesture. What early along needed explanation, now is intuitively known, accepted, and embraced. So, too, in our life of prayer: paragraphs give way to words that in turn give way to loving and expectant silence. It is not only the content of our prayer that changes as we age; the very manner of our praying also matures, like the communication between committed spouses or friends.

There is one more thing that changes over a lifetime of prayer: the image of God that we carry in our mind and treasure in our heart. We need always remember the difference between God and our image of God. Over a lifetime of prayer and because of our praying, the divine grace infused into our mind and heart by the Spirit of God slowly purifies our image of God and gradually transforms how we understand God to be. As our image and understanding of God evolve, we ourselves grow more and more into God's likeness and glory by the power of the Spirit (2 Cor 3:18).

101. The Hail Mary ends with a request of the Blessed Mother that she pray for us "now and at the hour of our death." How can I be sure that I will remain faithful to a life of prayer until my death?

Simply by praying for such perseverance. Remember the image of the expectant father in the parable of the prodigal son (Luke 15)? He scanned the horizon looking and hoping for the return of his wandering child. In this parable Jesus provides us just a glimpse of God's yearning for us. As we begin or continue our life of prayer, we need not worry about our shortcomings, doubts, or weaknesses. Nothing can keep us from the love that God has for us (Rom 8:39).

There is also the maternal image of God in the prophet Isaiah: "Can a woman forget her nursing child, or show no compassion for the child of her womb? Even these may forget, yet I will not forget you" (Isa 49:15). God's paternal and maternal instincts ensure that our names are in the divine memory forever. This covenant promise, together with the prayers of God's Mother Mary, is our hope and salvation.

There is a charming story in the Old Testament about prayer. It reminds us that whatever our age, wherever we are, however we find ourselves, God will not cease to come to us. In the First Book of Samuel we read how as a young boy Samuel did not understand that God had been speaking to him all through a long night of interrupted sleep. Assured by his guardian and mentor, the priest Eli, that God was indeed calling out to him, Samuel finally responded to God: "Speak, for your servant is listening" (1 Sam 3:10). These words of Samuel remind us that, at any age and in any circumstance, prayer is our response to God, who constantly calls out to us in different ways during our life. Fidelity in prayer is not so much a matter of our virtue as it is of God's infinite love for us. That love will never fail (1 Cor 13:8, 13).

Notes

1. These four ancient Christian writers reflected on the nature of prayer in their books, sermons, and letters. See especially: *The Confessions of Saint Augustine,* trans. Maria Boulding, OSB (Hyde Park, NY: New City Press, 1994); St. Augustine's *Sermons* 61 and 77B in *The Works of St. Augustine: Sermons III (51–94)* (Hyde Park, NY: New City Press, 1991); Richard Travers Smith, *St. Basil the Great* (Whitefish, MT: Kessinger Publishing, 2003); Andrew Louth, *St. John Damascene: Tradition and Originality in Byzantine Theology* (New York: Oxford University Press, 2004); and *John Climacus: The Ladder of Divine Ascent,* trans. Colm Luibheid and Norman Russell (Mahwah, NJ: Paulist Press, 1982).

2. *Confessions* I, 1, 1.

3. *Catechism of the Catholic Church* (Washington, DC: United States Catholic Conference, 1994), 2699, 2702. The entire text of the *Catechism* is also available at www.vatican.va, Resource Library, Catechism of the Catholic Church. Hereafter, the *Catechism* is abbreviated as *CCC.*

4. *CCC,* 2698.

5. *Spiritual Exercises* of St. Ignatius, 1. See *Ignatius of Loyola: Spiritual Exercises and Selected Works,* The Classics of Western Spirituality series, ed. George E. Ganss, SJ, with the collaboration of Jesuits Parmananda Divarkar, Edward J. Malatesta, and Martin E. Palmer (Mahwah, NJ: Paulist Press, 1991), 1.

6. *CCC,* 2565.

7. *Confessions* III, 6, 11.

8. *CCC,* 2846–2849.

9. *The Interior Castle,* IV, i, 3; V, iv, 4, 7. See *Teresa of Avila: The Interior Castle,* The Classics of Western Spirituality series, trans.

Kieran Kavanaugh, OCD, and Otilio Rodriguez, OCD (Mahwah, NJ: Paulist Press, 1979).

10. *Confessions* I, 13, 21.

11. Chandogya Upanishad, in *The Upanishads* (London: Penguin Classics, 1965), 63–78.

12. *CCC,* 2675.

13. *CCC,* 2683–2684.

14. *CCC,* 2626–2643.

15. *CCC,* 335.

16. *CCC,* 1471–1479.

17. Vatican Council II, *Constitution on the Sacred Liturgy (Sacrosanctum Concilium),* 10. For full text see www.vatican.va, Resource Library, II Vatican Council.

18. *Confessions* IX, 10, 23–26.

19. See the Old Testament Song of Songs also called the Song of Solomon, as well as the writings of St. Teresa of Avila and *Hildegard of Bingen: Scivias,* trans. Mother Columba Hart and Jane Bishop, introduction by Barbara Newman (Mahwah, NJ: Paulist Press, 1990).

20. See http://monasticdialog.com/a.php?id=67 for an instructive commentary on this event.

21. Vatican Council II, *The Relation of the Church to Non-Christian Religions (Nostra Aetate),* 2. For full text see www.vatican.va, Resource Library, II Vatican Council.

22. *Dynamics of Faith,* Paul Tillich (New York: Harper and Row, 1957), 26.

Glossary of Terms

adhan: The Islamic call to "Come to Prayer" that is sung five times each day by the muezzin, usually from the tower or minaret of the local mosque. It is also proclaimed at home and school for important events that invite prayer and praise. It is sung in Arabic and begins with the proclamation *Allahu Akbar,* God is Great and is worthy of worship.

atman–Brahman: Two Sanskrit words used in Hindu teaching about the soul and God. *Atman* refers to the soul or the deepest and most abiding spiritual element in every person. *Brahman* is the ancient word for the Holy One or God who is infinite and universal. In Hindu teaching these two are ultimately one and the same reality. Every soul emanates from God as a wave arises from the ocean. This Hindu teaching of the unity between the soul and God is different from the relationship of love between the soul and God found in Judaism, Christianity, and Islam.

bodhi: A Sanskrit word that means awake or enlightened. In Buddhism it refers to the state of awareness and happiness achieved by Gautama, the Buddha or Enlightened One. It is the goal of Buddhist practice. Once achieved, one is free from desire *(tanha)* and the suffering *(dukkha)* it causes.

Centering Prayer: A kind of Christian meditation that draws from the ancient practice of the Eastern desert monks and nuns who lifted their mind and heart to God through the constant repetition of a sacred word or phrase (mantra). This practice is also recommended in the anonymous, medieval work *The Cloud of Unknowing.* For the past thirty years Centering Prayer has been taught by the Cistercian or Trappist monks of St. Joseph's Abbey in Spencer, Massachusetts.

contemplation: A simple, quiet dwelling in the presence of God during which the mind and heart are filled with an abiding sense of the Holy One. In contemplation one moves beyond meditation on various themes or events and into a loving adoration of God. Contemplative moments can become part of one's daily prayer. Very intense contemplative experience may involve ecstasy.

Divine Office: See Liturgy of the Hours

ecstasy: An experience of moving out of (ex-) or beyond one's self. In prayerful ecstasy a person experiences the reality of God so strongly that a sense of individual self is overwhelmed or left behind during an immersion into the divine. People who experience frequent ecstasy are known as mystics.

grace: A religious teaching in Christianity and other religions that refers to the abiding, active, and healing presence and power of God in both individual and social experience. In Christian teaching God's grace climaxes in the person of Jesus of Nazareth.

icon: Two-dimensional paintings of Christ, the Trinity, Mary, and the angels and saints characteristic of Eastern or Orthodox Christianity. Known for their exquisite beauty and ancient tradition, icons are themselves created in a carefully proscribed process of prayer and fasting before the artist (who usually remains anonymous) begins "writing" the icon. The work of creating the icon is itself an act of prayer. The purpose of icons is to draw all who see them into the Divine Presence and so into prayerful relationship with God. Christians venerate icons, but do not worship them. They are aids, symbols, or invitations for the believer to worship God, or to petition the Virgin Mary, angels, or saints for their intercession. The Second Council of Nicea in 787 CE condemned the movement of iconoclasm and upheld the right of believers to respect and cherish sacred icons and images that nurture faith and prayer.

idol: A religious symbol or artifact that has itself become identified with the divine reality to which it points. Thus the golden calf, which the Book of Exodus says the Hebrews worshipped in the desert, is one of the first idols mentioned in the Bible. The Bible contrasts idolatry with worship of the one, true God who cannot be captured or represented in any way by human artifact. Judaism and Islam (especially Sunni sects) are especially wary of the temptation to idolatry and so discourage or even prohibit sacred images of any type. Christians, especially Catholic and Orthodox churches, value the proper role of icons and other sacred art as aids to prayer.

Kabbalah: The mystical, ecstatic tradition within Judaism. Its origins seem to be in early medieval rabbinic schools in Europe, but adherents trace the tradition of Kabbalah throughout the history of Hebrew scripture and subsequent rabbinic writings. It emphasizes the contemplative experience of God through Jewish belief and teaching.

Liturgy of the Hours (Divine Office): Also called the Prayer of Christians, it is the cycle of five daily prayers in Catholic liturgy: morning prayer, daytime prayer, evening prayer, night prayer, and the prayer of readings that can be done at any time of day or night. Psalms and other scriptural songs together with readings from scripture and prayers of petition and intercession comprise each of the Hours. The Hours are usually sung in monastic and religious communities, but all Christians are invited and encouraged to use this resource to enrich their lives of faith and prayer.

mantra: A word or phrase repeated many times during prayer as an aid to focus the mind and heart on God. A mantra can be vocal or silent, and is often coordinated with breathing. Mantras are recommended in many Hindu and Buddhist meditative practices and have also been part of Christian contemplative prayer, as in the ancient Jesus Prayer of Eastern Orthodox Christianity.

meditation: Prayer that engages the mind and heart by intentional reflection on sacred scripture; on the life of Jesus, Mary, or a saint; or on the events of one's life in the light of faith. Meditation moves from thoughtful reflection to affection, that is, to feelings of love, adoration, thanksgiving, sorrow, and joy in the presence of God.

mystic: A prayerful person who often experiences ecstasy as part of his or her life of meditation and contemplation.

novena: A Roman Catholic practice of the daily repetition of a prayer or set of prayers for nine consecutive days, usually for a particular petition or intercession. The tradition of the novena may have originated from the nine days the disciples spent in prayer between Jesus' ascension into heaven and the descent of the Holy Spirit at Pentecost.

orans: A Latin word that literally means praying. It refers to any icon, statue, or painting of the Virgin Mary, saints, or angels in an attitude of prayer, usually depicted by hands outstretched with palms facing up—an ancient Christian prayer posture.

pilgrimage: A journey made by an individual or group to a sacred destination. Prayer and meditation are important components of pilgrimage, as is a certain dependence upon God to provide food and shelter along the way.

prayer: Lifting up mind and heart to God or asking good things of God.

Prayer of Christians: See Liturgy of the Hours

psalms: The book or collection in the Old Testament or Hebrew Scriptures of 150 inspired songs and prayers, attributed to King

David. The psalms are used throughout Christian liturgical worship as well as in private devotion.

puja: Hindu rituals of worship and devotion practiced at temple or at home.

qibla: The direction of Mecca toward which Muslims are expected to pray five times each day. It is determined by Muslims around the world using different traditions and techniques.

Qur'an: The sacred text of divine guidance and direction revealed to the prophet Muhammad over a period of twenty-three years in the early seventh century. Muslims revere the original Arabic text as the very word of God.

Ramadan: The ninth month of the Islamic calendar observed as a time of fasting (from sunrise to sunset), of intensified prayer, and of attention to works of charity.

ritual: A proscribed set of words, symbols, and actions that make up the traditional public prayers or ceremonies of a religious group. Ritual forms characterize the liturgy or sacraments in Catholic, Orthodox, and certain Protestant denominations.

sacrament: The most important rituals of Christian liturgy. The Catholic Church celebrates seven sacraments (baptism, confirmation, Eucharist, reconciliation, holy orders, anointing of the sick, and marriage).

sacrifice: Literally means "to make holy." We sacrifice something when we set it aside for God, or dedicate it to God. Sacrifice is prayer to the extent that the sacrificial object and action help worshippers lift mind and heart to God and symbolize the request of good things from God.

Salat: The five daily prayers (just before dawn, at noon, in late afternoon, just after sunset, and before retiring) made by Muslims in response to the *adhan* or call to "Come to Prayer." The *Salat* is preceded by ceremonial washings and is a ritually complex sequence of bows, prostrations, and prayers that pull the whole believer, body and soul, into submission before God.

sandhya: In Hinduism the prayers at the three junctions *(sandhya)* of the day: night to morning, forenoon to afternoon, and evening to night. At each *sandhya* the devotee prays the sacred *Gayatri* mantra that comes from the ancient Vedas.

Seder: The ritual meal celebrated by Jews on the first night of Passover to commemorate the delivery of the Hebrews by God from slavery in Egypt to freedom as God's people.

spiritual director: A priest, religious, or lay person who serves as a companion, mentor, or guide to help another on the faith journey of spiritual discovery and growth.

Sufism: The mystical tradition of Islam that arose probably in the eighth century. Its diverse teachings and practices are united by a focus on the cultivation of divine love and beauty, as well as an openness to various paths of spirituality.

Tibetan Buddhism: The Buddhist teaching and practice characteristic of Tibet and the wider Himalayan region. Known for its elaborate rituals, monastic communities, meditation techniques, divination of spirits, and devotion to the spiritual leader known as the Dalai Lama, Tibetan Buddhism has spread around the world.

Trinity: The Christian doctrine of belief in God as three Persons—Father (Creator), Son (Redeemer), and Holy Spirit (Sanctifier)—in one divine nature. Belief in the Trinity emerges from New Testament faith in Jesus as the Son of God and in the gift of the Holy Spirit. It was developed as a doctrine in the early centuries of the Christian church, and is the context of Christian prayer.

Upanishads: Sections of the Vedas devoted to meditation on the nature of the Holy One or *Brahman.*

Vedas: The meditations and teachings of saints, mystics, and seers from the Indian subcontinent, containing thousands of prayers still used today among the many sects and devotions of Hinduism. The oldest written Veda comes from around 1500 BCE.

Word of God: Jewish, Christian, and Islamic belief that God has spoken and revealed the divine will through human agents such as the prophets. For Christians the Bible is the written record of the Word of God. In Jesus, the Word made flesh, and through his followers by the indwelling of the Holy Spirit, God's Word is a living and enduring reality in human history.

worship: The attitude and action of prayer, especially adoration, praise, and blessing, expressed by an individual privately, or shared by a group publicly or through the ritual traditions of a religion.

yoga: Ancient Hindu ascetic practices that originated in India as ways leading to an experience of *Brahman* or God. Each of the four major traditions of yoga has its own particular emphasis and tradition: *jnana* (knowledge), *bhakti* (devotion), *karma* (action or morality), and *raja* (philosophy). *Hatha* is yoga as physical and mental exercise.

Further Resources

The Classics of Western Spirituality series (Paulist Press) is a treasure trove of the spiritual writings from Catholic, Protestant, Orthodox, Jewish, Muslim, Sufi, Persian, and indigenous traditions. Over 100 texts present a depth and breadth of wisdom on faith and prayer (see www.paulistpress.com). The following selections may be of special interest:

Alphonsus de Liguori: Selected Writings, edited by Frederick M. Jones, CSSR.

Augustine of Hippo: Selected Writings, translated and introduced by Mary T. Clark.

The Cloud of Unknowing, edited and introduced by James Walsh.

Early Islamic Mysticism: Sufi, Qur'an, Mi'raj, Poetic and Theological Writings, translated, edited, and with an introduction by Michael A. Sells.

Hildegard of Bingen: Scivias, translated by Mother Columba Hart and Jane Bishop; introduction by Barbara Newman.

Ignatius of Loyola: Spiritual Exercises and Selected Works, edited by George E. Ganss, SJ, with the collaboration of Jesuits Parmananda Divarkar, Edward J. Malatesta, and Martin E. Palmer; preface by John W. Padberg, SJ.

John Cassian: Conferences, translated by Colm Luibheid; introduced by Owen Chadwick.

John Climacus: The Ladder of Divine Ascent, translation by Colm Luibheid and Norman Russell.

John of the Cross: Selected Writings, edited with an introduction by Kieran Kavanaugh, OCD.

Julian of Norwich: Showings, translated and introduced by Edmund Colledge, OSA, and James Walsh, SJ; preface by Jean Leclercq, OSB.

Knowledge of God in Classical Sufism: Foundations of Islamic Mystical Theology, translated and introduced by John Renard; preface by Ahmet T. Karamustafa.

Meister Eckhart: Teacher and Preacher, edited by Bernard McGinn with the collaboration of Frank Tobin and Elvira Borgstadt; preface by Kenneth J. Northcott.

Teresa of Avila: The Interior Castle, translated by Kieran Kavanaugh, OCD, and Otilio Rodriguez, OCD.

Zohar: The Book of Enlightenment, translation and introduction by Daniel Chanan Matt; preface by Arthur Green.

Other helpful texts on prayer, meditation, and contemplation:

Centering Prayer and Inner Awakening, by Cynthia Bourgeault, Cowley, 2004.

Centering Prayer: Renewing an Ancient Christian Prayer Form, by M. Basil Pennington, Image, 1982.

Children's Book of Bedtime Blessings, by Ellen J. Kendig, Paulist Press, 2000.

Children's Book of Family Blessings, by Ellen J. Kendig, Paulist Press, 1999.

The Confessions of Saint Augustine, translated by Maria Boulding, OSB, New City Press, 1994.

The Gift of Peace, by Joseph Cardinal Bernadin, Doubleday (Loyola), 1997.

Introduction to the Devout Life, by Francis de Sales, Vintage (Random House), 2002.

Lectio Divina, by M. Basil Pennington, Crossroad Classic, 1998.

Light Within: The Inner Path of Meditation, by Laurence Freeman, OSB, Crossroad Classic, 1987.

Prayer: A History, by Philip Zaleski and Carol Zaleski, Houghton Mifflin, 2006.

Prayer of Heart and Body: Meditation and Yoga as Christian Spiritual Practice, by Thomas Ryan, Paulist Press, 1995.

The Rule of Saint Benedict: A Commentary in Light of World Ascetic Traditions, by Mayeul de Dreuille, OSB, Paulist Press, 2002.

The School of Prayer: An Introduction to the Divine Office for All Christians, by John Brook, The Liturgical Press, 1991.

Helpful Web sites:

Christian meditation and contemplation: www.mediomedia.com

Mysticism: www.religiousworlds.com/mystic/whoswho.html

Spiritual direction: www.sdiworld.org/home.html

Science and faith: www.crosscurrents.org/polkinghorne

For *The Catechism of the Catholic Church* and II Vatican Council Documents: www.vatican.va/archive/index.htm

Scriptural Index

General Index